# ONLY LOVE CREATES

## The Spiritual Works of Mercy

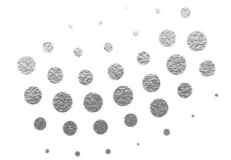

## FR. FABIO ROSINI

*Foreword by Msgr. Matteo Zuppi*
*Archbishop of Bologna*

*Translated by Robert J. Edmonson, CJ*

PARACLETE PRESS
BREWSTER, MASSACHUSETTS

2019 First Printing

*Only Love Creates: The Spiritual Works of Mercy*

English translation copyright © 2019 by Paraclete Press, Inc.

Originally published in Italian as *Solo l'amore crea: Le opere di misericordia spirituale*, copyright © 2016 by EDIZIONI SAN PAOLO s.r.l., Piazza Soncino 5 – 20092, Cinisello Balsamo (Milano), Italia. www.edizionisanpaolo.it. Used by permission.

ISBN 978-1-64060-111-6

Unless otherwise marked, Scripture references are taken from the *New Revised Standard Version Bible*, copyright 1989, Division of Christian Education of the National Council of the Churches of Christ in the United States of America. Used by permission. All rights reserved.

Scripture references marked (NJB) are from The New Jerusalem Bible, copyright © 1985 by Darton, Longman & Todd, Ltd., and Doubleday, a division of Random House, Inc. Reprinted by permission.

Translations of Italian texts quoted herein are the translator's own.

The Paraclete Press name and logo (dove on cross) are trademarks of Paraclete Press, Inc.

Library of Congress Cataloging-in-Publication Data

Names: Rosini, Fabio, author.
Title: Only love creates : the spiritual works of mercy / Fr. Fabio Rosini ;
    preface by Msgr. Matteo Zuppi, Archbishop of Bologna ; translated by
    Robert J. Edmonson, CJ.
Other titles: Solo l'amore crea. English
Description: Brewster, MA : Paraclete Press, Inc., 2018.
Identifiers: LCCN 2018025694 | ISBN 9781640601116 (trade paper)
Subjects: LCSH: Mercy. | Catholic Church--Doctrines.
Classification: LCC BV4647.M4 R6713 2018 | DDC 241/.4--dc23
LC record available at https://lccn.loc.gov/2018025694.

10 9 8 7 6 5 4 3 2 1

Published by Paraclete Press
Brewster, Massachusetts
www.paracletepress.com

Printed in the United States of America

# CONTENTS

I wrote this book during the first summer in which
both my father and my mother were no more.

This book is dedicated to them,
who are awaiting me in heaven,
and who waited for me so much,
too much, here on earth as well.

From them I had so many good convictions,
the best teachings,
even though with them I was brutish and poorly behaved,
I gave them pain, I offended them, and I wore out their patience.

But no one prayed for me more than they did.

None of this adds up.

# FOREWORD

These pages are written, but in reality, they speak. This book is completely in the style of Fr. Fabio—so direct, so exacting, so free of abrasiveness, so tender, that it makes us feel gently understood to the core, without letting anyone off lightly or compromising—like the love of God, which empties the heart of doubts that make us believe they are profound, but in reality they paralyze it. Reading it makes us hear the warm voice of Fr. Fabio, who speaks across the pages of the book, which are the fruit of the many encounters that he untiringly offers to so many, demonstrating that it is not young people who are the problem but rather our timidity and our mediocrity.

It is addressed to everyone: to priests and educators who, instead of binding themselves to Christ, worry about their role and their esteem; to parents who run away from responsibility; to Christians who are poisoned by places of common do-goodism, imitations and caricatures of true feelings and choices.

Mercy, indeed, is God's engagement, paid for at a high price, that carries us upward, makes us feel truly loved, and teaches us to find answers to the love of others, without fear and false respect. Mercy is freed from the false religion of individualism, in which I leave you alone, perhaps with proper politeness or with anonymous and aseptic virtual truths.

Mercy is to assume the burden of another, God's choice that becomes our choice, mine and yours at the same time.

This book is one of the fruits of this extraordinary Holy Year, and it helps us live mercy every day, causing us to hear God, who continues to show mercy. It helps us choose to do that with everyone, opening our eyes to see and understand the world and our neighbor. We are helped to discern, because not everything is mercy, and mercy is not reduced to the insipid molasses of good intentions, half-truths, facile and deceptive understandings that don't know how to indicate the paths of liberation and change!

Fr. Fabio helps us to unmask false identities and to reintroduce, in a personal manner, the works of mercy that are possible for all of us. He joins the corporal and spiritual acts of mercy. There is no distinction, and the former refer necessarily to the latter, freeing us from the temptation to be concerned for people only to offer some sort of response to the body but without looking at and helping the person, and vice versa.

This is mercy without paternalism and without letting people off lightly in order to attract some sort of buyer who is then inevitably disappointed. "One who knows how to tell me many beautiful things perhaps doesn't serve me much, but one who knows how to teach me to do beautiful things is truly useful to me," because "the center of mercy is not the lover and the lover's feelings, but the beloved and the beloved's true good."

In reality we can't live without mercy, leaving things gray, undefined, putting things off, being content to be a spectator, lounging on that couch that Pope Francis wants to make everyone get up from so that we won't lose our lives and so we can truly leave our mark on history.

Now, the mercy that Fr. Fabio helps us understand and live is the very mark that we can leave, ours and God's. Because "the deepest happiness in life is to care for another. Only real love gives real happiness."

There is in his reflections a great deal of God's Word and a great deal of humanity—namely, the good ground that the seed is seeking in order to bear fruit. And I thank Fr. Fabio because, as one who is attentive and knowledgeable about the Word, he helps us understand it, not with useless academics, in abstract or false moralizing, but with the sage humanity that this requires, because this is life, and he seeks only to generate a good life.

The simplicity of his speech and the essentiality he achieves clears away empty ritual. It is the fruit of so much prayer, of listening, of concern for working on the great harvest and talking about Jesus, *whether the time is favorable or unfavorable*, but always with so much passion—an "expert in humanity," as Paul VI used to say. "God's mercy seeks out our poverty and loves it. And our poverty, once it is loved, becomes mercy."

These pages help us understand and live what Pope Francis wrote in article 310 of *Amoris laetitia*:

> Mercy . . . is not sheer romanticism or a lukewarm response to God's love, which always seeks what is best for us, for "mercy is the very foundation of the Church's life. All of her pastoral activity should be caught up in the tenderness which she shows to believers; nothing in her preaching and her witness to the world can be lacking in mercy." It is true that at times "we act as arbiters of grace rather than its facilitators. But the Church is not a tollhouse; it is the house of the Father, where there is a place for everyone, with all their problems."

This book helps us know the beauty of the Father's house and to make it known to so many, not in the abstract, but with "works." And to *do* mercy.

I am writing these words on the day of the commemoration of St. Francis, a man of exceptionally human and exceptionally strong mercy for everyone, and precisely for that capacity to transform the wolf into a companion who was beloved by his very victims and reconciled with them.

In his *Admonitions*, which bear the echo of the speeches he gave to his friars in the last years of his life, we read:

Where there is love and wisdom,
There is no fear or ignorance.
Where there is patience and humility,
There is no anger or disturbance.
Where there is poverty with gladness,
There is no greed or envy.
Where there is quiet and meditation,
There is no toil or self-indulgence.
Where there is the love of the Lord to watch over his house,
There the enemy cannot find an entrance.
Where there is mercy and discreetness,
There is no excess or harshness.

—Msgr. Matteo Zuppi
    Archbishop of Bologna

# TRANSLATOR'S NOTE

This book was written in an informal Italian style that appeals to ordinary people. Rendering that style into English calls for a similar informal style.

Many thanks to these generous Italians who provided explanations of some of the idioms used in the Italian original: Demetrio Yocum, Livia Caprara, and Antonio Bruni.

—ROBERT J. EDMONSON, CJ

# INTRODUCTION

Going about as if on tiptoe, hoping not to bother anyone, I gathered the courage to talk about the works of spiritual mercy. I did that in a series of programs on Vatican Radio, while I was also explaining it to the young people of the Diocese of Rome, in a monthly experience agreed on by some assistant parish priests. Nowadays these works seem questionable, futile, if not reprehensible. We are in a time of practicality, of efficiency, of goods and services, of nonprofit organizations, of volunteerism, of charities, of results, of statistics. . . .

Perhaps we can serenely put into storage, into the closet of "religious" people, this trace of spirituality that this worthy world of social activism can't do without.

A friend of mine was telling me that one Christmas Eve he had gone to bring assistance to a series of homeless people in Rome, together with other sympathetic helpers from a Catholic movement. When he finished his rounds, he noticed that he still had time to go to Midnight Mass, and he happily blurted out: "Great! We'll make it on time to Mass!" The other four in the car turned their heads, astonished: "Mass?!" This wasn't on their program. It didn't interest them. They were sympathizers with the Catholic movement, but they didn't go to Mass, not even at Christmas. For Christmas they had just visited some homeless people, giving up their big Christmas family dinner.

Maybe they're right. Maybe there's no need for any spiritual works of mercy, nor for prayer, nor for Christmas Masses. Or maybe that's not true.

I've been a parish priest, and I've often been beside the beds of the dying. I've tried to celebrate almost every single funeral of the parishioners, having to give that up only when I really couldn't be present, because I was quite willing to celebrate Mass there. This is a perspective that has dug deeply into me, illuminated me, made me walk

1

within my heart. This is a moment in which everything is reduced to zero, in which friendships and family relationships appear bare and lacking. Grief is real, authentic, and you can't call it idiotic. This must be because I gave my first homily at the funeral of my brother, who had died in an airplane crash; this must be because the first sacrament that I administered as a priest was the anointing of the sick to my father, who had let a tumor in his stomach get worse just to be present at my ordination the first day, and he was on his way to having his stomach taken out since it had by now been compromised. But I thank God for having this indicator: what causes the most suffering is not the body but the heart. It isn't grief but senselessness. It isn't death but loneliness.

The spiritual works of mercy are concerned with the heart, with lack of meaning, with loneliness.

Someone in the past thought the most urgent thing for humanity is the satisfaction of our material needs. After listening to that person, we felt we should pick up the pieces of entire societies that were dehumanized because they were despiritualized.

Recently in front of my church there was a Bulgarian tramp. I had asked him what he wanted, and I seemed to understand that he wanted to go back to his mother's home. My knowledge of Bulgarian has its limits. But I organized the trip for him. After ten days or so he came back. Then some splendid young men came from the diocesan Caritas benevolent society and talked to us. They took him to a hostel. And so he had a bed to sleep in and a place to wash and eat. Sometimes he slept there, but then he ran away and camped out again in front of my church. He greeted me happily, calling me by name every time I came and went. He asked very little of me, and was almost always drunk.

I hardly understand a word of Bulgarian, but I succeeded in understanding what he wanted. He wanted me to stop and speak with him. He wanted me to know his name. His name was Georgi. The other day they made him leave on a plane for Bulgaria, a second time. I don't know if he'll come back again. It isn't easy to chat with Georgi. So that's why I wrote this book.

# MERCY AND ITS IMITATIONS

Let's start off by asking ourselves some questions. What is our balance sheet like with regard to compassionate love? Do we achieve a satisfactory amount of mercy? Does the world in which we take part possess a legal number for calling ourselves a merciful world? Certainly, it's a world that talks a lot about good feelings, that celebrates generosity, that flies the flag of solidarity, tolerance, acceptance. At the same time, it laments injustice and denounces cruelty and oppression. And indeed, two spectacular opposites exist: "social" on the one hand, "horror" on the other.

Let's take note that we are in a confused, contradictory world, one that gives with one hand and takes with the other, that cures with one and cuts to pieces with the other.

Does this mean we're facing a struggle between good and evil, and therefore between mercy and cruelty? Between good people and bad people?

Psalm 136, as we will see, repeats a phrase that's found quite frequently in the Bible: "for his mercy endures forever." There exists his mercy, that of God, which endures forever. And other mercies exist as well, mercies that know little about enduring forever. They have limits; they end. They can be overcome; they can be broken into pieces. Incomplete mercies. Offal of mercy. Sentimentalism, welfarism, do-goodism. They crash against the wall of the legal system; they land on the slogan of "This is too much!" And they fail.

In the meantime, evil is never completely like that. It has motives; it begins with laying claims; it's the fruit of a story. It's curious that in general it's interwoven with justice; it has a story to tell; it has a rage that justifies itself. It's motivated by a feeling of revenge; it remembers a love that's broken to pieces, a good thing that's shattered, a life that's stolen.

Feelings. Powerful, violent. I pick up a gun and I kill everybody, because when I was eleven years old I was smashed by a bully. I take an airplane and I bring down a skyscraper, because you bombed my village. So I take you, and all those like you, and I put you in Guantanamo and I interrogate you for 180 hours, with a freezing cell and waterboarding. I'm right. I'm doing the righteous thing. *Gott mit uns.*

What is the lever, the fulcrum of all that? Nothing good and bad. Only vision that's partial, unilateral, disintegrated, individualistic, even if it has some aspects that are justified.

What we ought to be talking about is something completely different. It's called works of mercy, or even works of everlasting life. The word *everlasting*—in Greek *aiôn*, in Hebrew *olam*—in every language implies a meaning of completeness, of absence of limits, with acceptance of entirety. Works that are complete. Mercy without errors in the source code. What errors? We will see.

## MERCY ISN'T A FEELING

Love is not a feeling. No, it isn't. In itself it would be an action. Being the most complicated and most profound thing a two-footed creature can do, love is interwoven with the entire person and therefore also with the feelings. But if it were only a feeling, it would obey the confines of feelings. And instead, love often asks us also to travel in other territories. Such as every time we do something we have no desire to do, something that's only for the other person, strictly for their good. No, rocking a baby who wakes you up for the fourth time during the same night, even if it's the fifth consecutive night of the same thing, isn't done on the strength of a feeling; it's done only for the child. Feelings? Not after the second night on. Perhaps the feeling of amazement at not having done the child in, they tell me.

Mercy also suffers these false identities—as often happens with the cornerstones of Christian life, amid generic understandings, unadvisable shortcuts in logic, and the tendency toward small superficialities, the question is at least put on the table. It will be better to draw on the genuine and primordial facts of Sacred Scripture.

And here we humbly take note that mercy is an argument that's too vast to be circumscribed. Let's resign ourselves to the fact that we will only be able to identify its principal characteristics. Two of them, as we will see.

What is mercy in Scripture? If we stubbornly maintain that it's an emotional/interior state of the one who shows it, a sense of compassion, of forgiveness and acceptance, that addresses the other when they're in need and when they're in error, we're missing the mark. According to this line, God would be the first one to display this attitude when we find ourselves in certain situations, or when we come up short. He'd use being merciful and forgiving when faced with human error and weakness. Or so they say. Such forgiveness, truth be told, seems like a sort of conditional amnesty that's behind God's patience. Humans make mistakes, and yet God forgives.

Then we in turn ought to be merciful. How? For consistency, by obeying a noble sort of duty and commitment of will. Goodbye to sentiments. The minimum risk, seeing what the word *duty* involves, is of sounding false, if it's true that mercy is a movement of the heart.

Simplistic. Misleading. What can we take as our starting point?

The fundamental terms that express mercy in the Old Testament can be found in an indispensable text from the thirty-fourth chapter of the book of Exodus, where the Lord proclaims his own Name with an abundance of attributes that had not been expressed until that moment in Scripture.

The immediate background concerns Moses, the man who experienced an extraordinary revelation of God and of his name, and on the basis of this revelation lived through an epic work, that of the liberation of the people from Egypt. After they arrived at the foot of Mount Sinai, after the opening of the Red Sea and their passage through the desert, a covenant was entered into. This covenant was soon betrayed by the people—we remember the golden calf— and there was a need to restore the relationship between God and the people. New tablets of stone were forged with the Ten Commandments of the covenant, so we were ready for the Lord to pass before the people and for Moses to proclaim his name, because from his name derives the potential to make things new and reestablish what has been broken. The text reads,

> The LORD, the LORD,
> a God merciful and gracious,
> slow to anger,
> and abounding in steadfast love and faithfulness,
> keeping steadfast love for the thousandth generation,
> forgiving iniquity and transgression and sin,
> yet by no means clearing the guilty,
> but visiting the iniquity of the parents
> upon the children
> and the children's children,
> to the third and the fourth generation. (Exod. 34:6–7)

Merciful, compassionate, slow to anger, rich in grace and faithfulness. This is his identity card. As we said, the God of the Bible had never been so talkative about his own attitudes. For example, let's think about the expression *slow to anger*. Let's try to put a speedometer on our snapshots of anger. . . .

*Rich in love and faithfulness*: God is rich, rich in love, St. Paul would say—"God, who is rich in mercy . . ." (Eph. 2:4). This is his richness. There are people who are rich in qualities, in ideas, in goods, in money; he is rich in mercy. When he wants to speak about himself, he doesn't say, "How strong I am, how good I am, how beautiful I am, how right I am." He could well say that, but instead he affirms: "I am mercy," "I am patience, I am slow to anger." And we understand that this is a huge thing: that between the identity of God himself and his mercy, his compassion, his grace, and his faithfulness, there is a perfect coinciding. God is not merciful a few times, when it's worth it: his nature is mercy. And so it will ever be.

However, those other expressions that follow immediately seem to clash: they speak of "punishment" and "chastening." Why? What do they have to do with mercy? One thing at a time.

Two fundamental Hebrew terms, the first two attributes used in this text, give us the key to understanding the biblical verses on mercy.

The first, translated in our version as "mercy," in Hebrew *hesed*, is the term used most often in the Bible to indicate God's love, his tenderness, his posture toward humanity. What is *hesed*?

As an example, Psalm 136, which was mentioned earlier, repeats an obsessive number of times, twenty-six of them, the same phrase, which in Hebrew is *ki le-olam hasdò*: "for his mercy endures forever," or, in some translations, "his love endures forever."

This psalm talks about a series of things that God does because "his mercy endures forever." For example, in the first four verses we read:

> O give thanks to the LORD, for he is good,
>> for his steadfast love endures forever.
> O give thanks to the God of gods,
>> for his steadfast love endures forever.
> O give thanks to the Lord of lords,
>> for his steadfast love endures forever;
> who alone does great wonders,
>> for his steadfast love endures forever;

Up to this point there is nothing disconcerting. But then verses 5 and 6 follow:

> who by understanding made the heavens,
>> for his steadfast love endures forever;

7

who spread out the earth on the waters,
>	for his steadfast love endures forever;

He created the world . . . out of mercy? If mercy is understood as a response to the sinfulness and the wretchedness of humans, what are we talking about here, seeing that humans had not yet been created? Therefore, mercy is seen in relationship to creation. This is less clear here.

A bit later, in verses 10 and 11, the psalm says,

who struck Egypt through their firstborn,
>	for his steadfast love endures forever;
and brought Israel out from among them,
>	for his steadfast love endures forever;

In delivering the people from Egypt, he was exercising his merciful love. We understand this more because of our experience of redemption from the oppression of sin and evil. God frees his people from this wretched condition because "his mercy endures forever." He looked upon the misery of an oppressed people. He turns toward us all the more.

But let's go on further in this psalm and we discover, in verse 25, that he "gives food to all flesh, for his steadfast love endures forever." That is, God is still at work today, providing for all creatures out of his mercy, just as he created the world out of his mercy and redeems his people out of his mercy.

Three fundamental junctions: Creation, Redemption, and Providence. The world was created out of mercy, the people experienced liberation through mercy, and the world is under a merciful conduct of present history. What are we talking about if we touch on Creation, Redemption, Providence? Broadly speaking, we are talking about . . . everything.

God is always operating according to his mercy because mercy is his nature. Therefore, if we want to understand this term, we should affirm that it's the loving-kindness of God that's nonetheless made explicit in faithfulness and operativeness: God displays his *hesed*, his mercy, by doing something with us. He isn't showing an occasional sentiment; this is the impulse that guides *each* of his works, all that he does for humankind. His is a faithful tenderness, one that governs, carries through, creates, guides history. It's his solicitude toward humanity that's connected to his faithfulness that he is and has toward us. Therefore, this term places us before a Father who doesn't abandon us, a Father who is merciful no matter what he does with us; and we begin to understand that also when he corrects us, when he tells us no, when he reproaches us, he's involving himself with us. Love, mercy, appear here as an operative given, not based on sentiment, that touches on the facts and doesn't remain in the heart of those who are merciful, but effectively touches the lives of those who are the objects of mercy.

## "VISCERAL" LOVE FOR THE OTHER

Let's go on to the second term used in Exodus 34:6: the lexical unit *raham*, used less than *hesed* but likewise fundamental in Scripture. It comes from the verb and the noun related to "viscera," "uterus." It's a type of love linked to the capacity to carry a child in the womb. We have therefore passed from a paternal/masculine aspect, the caring male tenderness, to a typically maternal/feminine term, where the capacity to conceive life appears.

We must break free from our mentality in which the term *mercy* is linked to the word *heart*—in Latin *misereor* (compassion) and *cor-cordis* (heart)—and thereby relativize our vision linked to that organ, the heart, which pulsates and beats, and which emotion speeds up but fear stops.

Moving away from our cardiac approach to mercy, we enter into the Hebrew language in which leverage is drawn from the only human organ that's capable of "gestating" life. It's the human organ that's completely dedicated to the life of another, the one that ushers in that specific care that's wholly feminine—that unrepeatable, splendid maternal trait that's the capacity to safeguard life, feed it, take care of it, "pamper" it, and from which derives the fact that throughout history women have always killed less than men. Women don't possess the physical strength of men; they don't run as fast as men; they don't jump higher than men. But whereas to men is reserved the characteristic of fertilizing, from causing to go forth, of knowing how to trigger, and that's the genius of men; by contrast the capacity to embrace, accept, and welcome, to give birth, to nurture, to safeguard, to grow, is wholly feminine. Men can conceive of the idea of killing; for women this is much more difficult—apart from the modern terrifying plague of abortion that opens an unheard-of chapter in the history of humanity.

God's love, surprisingly, is visceral, certainly not in the sense of being impetuous or attributable to the emotions, but of being analogous to what in the female womb creates another person. If we have experienced God's forgiveness concerning a grave sin, we realize that this forgiveness is not a single, one-time absolution; it causes us to be reborn; it gives us a fresh start. It makes all things new.

God's mercy has within itself both fatherliness and motherliness. One passage of Scripture says:

Can a woman forget her nursing child,
   or show no compassion for the child of her womb?
Even these may forget,
   yet I will not forget you. (Isa. 49:15)

Psalm 103:7–13 says:

He made known his ways to Moses,
   his acts to the people of Israel.
The LORD is merciful and gracious,
   slow to anger and abounding in steadfast love.
He will not always accuse,
   nor will he keep his anger forever.

He does not deal with us according to our sins,
    nor repay us according to our iniquities.
For as the heavens are high above the earth,
    so great is his steadfast love (*hesed*) toward those who fear him;
as far as the east is from the west,
    so far he removes our transgressions from us.
As a father has compassion (*raham*) for his children,
    so the Lord has compassion for those who fear him.

Here, God actively carries out within us a work: to take away our faults. he's tender because he knows out of what we are modeled, and he remembers that we are so fragile.

Mercy is not that type of reality that has as its theme the state of soul of the one who loves, but is centered on the life of the one who is loved. Love is a work, not an interior motive. If it remains such, it's an inclination without truth, without reality, without obedience to the real needs of the one who is loved. Love does good to the beloved, with paternal robustness and maternal tenderness, caring for the other, providing for, sustaining, caring for, giving new prospects, new possibilities. God's love is like that: it's a love that knows what you are made of, how weak you are, why you have fallen, and provides for you, taking you away from your faults.

Does this mean that he always proves you right? Absolutely not! Love, for example, corrects, as is testified to by Deuteronomy 8:5: "Know then in your heart that as a parent disciplines a child so the Lord your God disciplines you." By this we understand how God in Exodus 34:7 reveals his love, reveals a love that doesn't leave us to ourselves, a love that leads us to be cared for by him, corrected by him. Here is why: God is

by no means clearing the guilty,
but visiting the iniquity of the parents
upon the children

and the children's children,
to the third and the fourth generation.

In an archaic but deep way, considering how much the correction of a skewed structure is difficult, this text expresses how necessary it is never to read a human problem as an individual problem. Today modern psychodynamics is increasingly taking note that discomfort is always social. A psychotherapist friend used to say to me: "In order to help the dis-ease of a young man, I would have to put the whole family through therapy, from the great-grandfather if he were alive, all the way down, and then all of his classmates and his roommates. . . . We work as if there existed a dis-ease, a discomfort, that can be taken out of context!"

Whatever the case may be, we need a constant therapy of correction and growth.

It's interesting to note that in the New Testament, the song of the Blessed Virgin Mary, the *Magnificat*, is a song about God's works, of his baring his arm, and of his mighty works. This text proclaims God's mercy, citing it in the opening and the closing of the part of the song that describes God's style in carrying out his work. Mary talks with Elizabeth and sings:

My soul magnifies the Lord,
    and my spirit rejoices in God my Savior,
for he has looked with favor on the lowliness of his servant.
    Surely, from now on all generations will call me blessed;
for the Mighty One has done great things for me,
    and holy is his name.

Now come the specifics of how the Lord will do his great works:

His mercy is for those who fear him
    from generation to generation.
He has shown strength with his arm;
    he has scattered the proud in the thoughts of their hearts.

He has brought down the powerful from their thrones,
  and lifted up the lowly;
he has filled the hungry with good things,
  and sent the rich away empty.
He has helped his servant Israel,
  in remembrance of his mercy,
according to the promise he made to our ancestors,
  to Abraham and to his descendants forever. (Lk. 1:46–55)

Therefore, mercy includes this second part of the text and has a style. Which?

He has shown strength with his arm;
  he has scattered the proud in the thoughts of their hearts.
He has brought down the powerful from their thrones,
  and lifted up the lowly.

So, mercy is what brings down the powerful from their thrones? It scatters the proud in the thoughts of their hearts? In life, if God did not permit certain humiliations, certain bitternesses, who could take a step back and say, "What have I done? How am I living?" Who would have ever entered back within oneself, if love had not challenged us, unmasked us without holding back?

Mercy holds me fast, knows how precious I am, doesn't abandon me. It seeks out that one sheep that has become lost and goes searching for us until it finds it. God doesn't want to lose a single person, and there is no one about whom God says, "Without you it's all the same; things can be done without you." How many people have we left on the road of our lives? We have said, "With that one over there we have lost our patience." God doesn't do that: his mercy is constant, faithful. A mother, if one of her children falls away, never gives up. She searches for her child. In every way.

God's mercy is that which comforts us when we need it, but it knows to slap us, to correct us, to take care of us by standing against us.

People who have done us good perhaps have had to speak to us with all due toughness. Love is not a mollusk! Love is strong and powerful, and it affects us. If love were a feeling, it would move nothing, and we would all remain in a sloppy swill of soul. Does a true friend see you as you are and what you are doing and remain aloof? Will that friend not stand against you if that's what you need? Will that friend not dirty his or her hands with you? Who is a good father? One who gives into everything? Or one who, without exacerbating the problem, knows how to correct his own children and bring them to their true good?

One time I was talking with some adolescents about the temptations of Christ in the desert and about the fact that in the case of the pinnacle of the temple, we are all photographed in the pretense that God moves with our times, that he always does what we ask him. I once asked a fourteen-year-old girl, "What would you think if your father always did what you ask him?" She sat quietly for a moment and then answered, "That he didn't love me anymore." She was right. One who loves you tells you, "No." One who loves you challenges you, corrects you. Logically that's not all they do, but they know when it's needed.

God's mercy is his care over our lives, because mercy is attentiveness toward another, and the pursuit of the good of another. Mercy requires us to know with tenacity and tenderness how to seek the best for the other, accompany the other to their most beautiful dimension, support that person toward the good, and guide them, if the opportunity arises.

One who knows how to tell me many beautiful things perhaps doesn't serve me well, but one who knows how to teach me to do beautiful things is truly useful to me.

No, there's no doubt: mercy is an action, it's work, it's wisdom, it's care, it's a healthy concern that doesn't let up until it has helped the other toward a good result. It's to know how to uphold, and therefore to watch out for the other, and to shout if needed, knowing how to say yes or no; it doesn't depend on what it "feels," but on what serves the other the best.

The center of mercy is not the one who loves and his or her feelings, but the beloved and that one's true good. If all we have is the lover and narcissism, that's merely aesthetics.

God loves us by correcting us when we need it, comforting us when we need it, endorsing and supporting us when we need it, and putting us in front of walls if we need it. He knows what we are made of, and he knows that without him we won't make it. Just as a father corrects his children, and as a mother is always a "yes" for our life, no matter what we have done.

And above all, God never discourages us and never lets up his grip, "for his mercy endures forever."

But where does this take us? Fatherhood that provides, motherhood that generates and creates. These are prerogatives that have to do with life. These are not ethical categories, but rather biological or existential ones. Being born, being brought up, upheld, cared for, healed, cured, protected, guided.

The perspective is that of one who takes by the hand and leads a child—his or her child. Fruit of his body, her womb, pupil of his or her eye. This is the God of the Bible, not of some sort of generic divine power, but the God of life. God's mercy points to an essential connection with the whole: life. Human life is precious. We are born in God, and only God possesses the characteristics of one who causes life to spring forth and guides it.

To say that mercy isn't a feeling isn't just to give a definition that saves us from emotionalism, but it means we must open ourselves to a deeper dimension. Mercy can't be copied, because an analogy about life can't be worked up. What would analogy with life be?

Let's attempt to analyze the phrase from the Gospel of Luke that would bind us to an apparent act of mimicking: "Be merciful, just as your Father is merciful" (Lk. 6:36).

Before any activity that's comparable to that of God comes relationship with God: the relationship of a child to a parent. Mercy doesn't spring forth from humans but from our relationship with God.

In a book this can't be done, but here we ought to repeat this sentence at least five times:

Mercy doesn't spring forth from humans but from our relationship with God.

Mercy doesn't spring forth from my will but from my relationship with God.

Mercy doesn't spring forth from my psychology but from my relationship with God.

Mercy doesn't spring forth from my energy but from my relationship with God.

Can this be done? Will the publisher, in their wisdom, allow it? Mercy, being interwoven with the capacity to generate and conduct life, ought to have, like life, its source in God.

This is why we fail.

Because we start from ourselves.

This is why we should repeat obsessively that mercy isn't a feeling, because it isn't a prerogative or a personal characteristic but the fruit of a relationship.

And now what? The mercy we are talking about isn't a human work; we described that human work at the beginning of the chapter as being incomplete, partial, and unsuccessful. What we should be talking about is the fruit of a synergy, or, better still, it's a work of God in humans. But it isn't magic; it implies human consent, human participation. The works of mercy are the actualization—the putting into practice in the here and now—of one of the theological virtues, charity. They're the work of the Holy Spirit in us. Otherwise we aren't talking about works of eternal life.

In fact, in dealing with the individual works of spiritual mercy, we ought to focus on imitations, para-works, and false, knock-off mercy. That's the most prevalent kind. True mercy is very rare.

# THE CORPORAL
# AND SPIRITUAL
# WORKS OF MERCY

Mercy isn't only the nature of God. It's also one of our dramatic urgencies. Let's try to think of a marriage without mercy, a friendship or a work environment without mercy. That's hell. Like a son who has no mercy for his father: "Let my father die alone like a dog. That bastard never really accepted me—now let him pay!" Are those scenarios unheard of?

Or yet let's imagine a fatherhood with a false, hypocritical, unreal mercy. The fictitious love of so many relationships that are never made clear, never truly intertwined until they touch the heart. That distance of one millimeter from the truth that seems a galaxy of difference. An unmentionable sadness, that of never having told everything, even to ourselves, of having left things gray, undefined.

Still more, can human beings draw deep in its roots the line of their own existence, while accepting the balance sheet of never having been really loved? Does mercy belong to the optional or to the necessities of human life?

The deepest happiness in life is to care for another. Try it to believe it. Only real love gives real happiness.

At the bedsides of so many dying ones I've comprehended that at the end of life the question arises whether we have truly loved another to the fullest. That's the question we will ask ourselves. We will become aware of not having run on empty if we have the certainty that we gave joy to someone, that we seriously cared for someone.

## MERCY: GOD'S WORK IN HUMANITY

So then we can ask ourselves: how do we do that? Where does this commoditiy come from? What are the works of mercy? How are they manifested? How do we go about caring for another? What is the way of doing it? These seem like obvious questions, but in reality we ought once again to probe some misconceptions.

Generally, as we have seen, we believe that mercy springs forth from the will, from the decision to be merciful, and we correlate that style, that approach, with duty: it's duty that calls us, that imposes on us to be merciful. People refer to mercy and to carrying out acts of compassion, forgiveness, acceptance, on the basis of "deciding to," "realizing that it's necessary to," "it's my duty."

That type of approach brings us to existential apnea, sliding into considering mercy, love, as a tiresome thing, a duty, for the carrying out of which we must be in an optimal physical and mental state, seeing that it requires our strength, our consistency, our commitment. As a result, we arrive at a considerable number of people who renounce the practice of mercy because they find it exhausting, burdensome. Forgiveness and service in fact live in apnea: I'll hold my breath after an act of mercy, turning in the end to being concerned about my life after having been concerned for another, while going without oxygen. . . .

All this doesn't square up; it corresponds to sad spiritual bankruptcy, to occasional stutterings of mercy—acts not carried to completion, parables not narrated but graphic, in which we start out to do something, but then we stop because we're tired, or we just can no longer make it. That's the trajectory of many volunteers who want to do things and discover that they're doing them out of their own strength, but their strength is small. How do we get out of this impasse?

In chapter two of Mark's Gospel something symbolic happens. Jesus is in Peter's house, and there are many people present, among whom are scribes. Some people who want to take a paralytic to reach Jesus can't get close to him. In those days houses had roofs made of a kind of straw or thatch, and these men, upon climbing up to the roof, made a hole in the roof through which they dropped down the paralytic on a stretcher and placed him in front of Jesus. What would we say about that? What is the urgency of this situation? A man is dropped down from a roof because he's a paralytic, there is no doubt—they carry him there because he can't walk. This is the problem.

Jesus observes the scene and says, "Son, your sins are forgiven" (Mk. 2:5).

What? What is going on? As if to a desperate man who had crossed the desert and arrived exhausted by thirst, we said, "Do you want friendship?" The paralytic can't walk; his problem is w-a-l-k-i-n-g! Jesus says, "Your sins are forgiven." But what is he saying? Has he understood the situation?

"Now some of the scribes were sitting there, questioning in their hearts, 'Why does this fellow speak in this way? It is blasphemy! Who can forgive sins but God alone?'" (Mk. 2:6–7). The scribes are right; they're saying a reasonable thing: Who can treat sin? We know how to wash a garment, regenerate material, clean and reclaim various things, but how do you clean a heart? How can a soul be wiped clean of an error? Stay there; it's got you—live with it. You can sublimate it or detach it or reinterpret it, but it stays there. To reset the counter of sins back to zero isn't in the reach of human technology.

In the Old Testament there are two verbs, "create" and "forgive," that have a single subject, God. "Create," in Hebrew *barà* (to extract from nothing), says that only God can create—this is undeniable. The other verb, *selah*, is to forgive—and this is also something only God can do. Who can say that our sins are remitted? What psychoanalyst can say that? God can give us a new life; only he knows how to do that. The scribes are right.

The scribes' problem is rather that they don't understand who they're dealing with. They're dealing with the very power of God:

At once Jesus perceived in his spirit that they were discussing these questions among themselves; and he said to them, "Why do you raise such questions in your hearts? Which is easier, to say to the paralytic, 'Your sins are forgiven,' or to say, 'Stand up and take your mat and walk'? But so that you may know that the Son of Man has authority on earth to forgive sins"—he said to the paralytic—"I say to you, stand up, take your mat and go to your home." And he stood up, and immediately took the mat and went out before all of them; so that they were all amazed and glorified God, saying, "We have never seen anything like this!"
—Mark 2:8–12

Jesus doesn't deny that only God can forgive sins, but he says, "the Son of Man has authority on earth to forgive sins"—in other words, he carries this power on earth.

God's mercy is God's alone. We can't administer its nature; we can't take possession of it. We can't ask mortals for God's mercy; we have to ask God for it. People can be "channels" of God's power. If by mercy we understand a cheap feeling, then a human can produce it; if by mercy we mean only a good intention, then, for what it's worth, a human can possess it; but in order for this thing to reach a successful conclusion, then what is required is the capacity to create, to have an impact on reality, as only God can do.

But how does the fruition, the transmission, of that mercy work? Let's go to the scene of Jesus's resurrection in John 20:19–23:

Jesus came and stood among them and said, "Peace be with you." After he said this, he showed them his hands and his side. Then the disciples rejoiced when they saw the Lord. Jesus said to them again, "Peace be with you. As the Father has sent me, so I send you." When he had said this, he breathed on them and said to them, "Receive the Holy Spirit. If you forgive the sins of any, they are forgiven them; if you retain the sins of any, they are retained."

Let's focus on one fact: as the Father sends Christ, so Christ sends us, giving us his Spirit.

Let's put our minds to this: Why does Jesus know how to love? Because he's loved. He is, and he lives in, a gift—namely, that the Father begot him, gave him being, gave him all of himself. The Son is happy to be; he's a joyful debtor; he experiences gratitude toward the Father. He's happy to be loved, and therefore his life is to love. Let's think about Jesus's baptism in the river Jordan: God reduces his distance to zero and interrupts, saying, "You are my Son, the Beloved; with you I am well pleased" (Mk. 1:11). Jesus contemplates that love, that joy, and he's happy with it. He does nothing without the Father. For him—think about it—to enter into our condition of sinners was, at Gethsemane, to prepare himself for separation from the Father. This was dramatic, frightful, so much so that he cried out, "My God, my God, why have you forsaken me?" (Mk. 15:34). He shouted, "How can I make it without You?"

Just think about how many things we do quite calmly without the Father. . . .

To receive the Holy Spirit means, first of all, to have the being of Christ, who is in relationship with the Father, to live in him, and to be full of gratefulness.

Forgiveness of sins, mercy according to the character of God, is the capacity to change a life, to give it a radical, new impulse; and this is a work of God. We can fail only if we set mercy above our will, above our decision, or above the sense of duty. These things can only be a poor foretaste. It's God's power alone that can work this regeneration.

There should also happen to us something that happened to Jesus. Just as he was moved, was sent, so also we need to live, to move, driven by the same motive, sent in a similar way.

"As the Father has sent me, so I send you" (John 20:21).

What are we talking about?

In John 13:23–25 there is a person called "the beloved disciple," who at the Last Supper makes a gesture and reclines his head on Jesus's chest. At that moment he has an intimate dialogue with Jesus concerning Judas's betrayal:

> One of his disciples—the one whom Jesus loved—was reclining next to him; Simon Peter therefore motioned to him to ask Jesus of whom he was speaking. So while reclining next to Jesus, he asked him, "Lord, who is it?"

In that moment he feels Jesus's heart beat with love for Judas. It's from that moment that he's called "the beloved disciple," not before, because he encountered love. "He reclined his head on the chest" of Jesus: that expression had already appeared at the end of the prologue at the beginning of John's Gospel, where there is an extraordinary hymn that, toward the end, says, "No one has ever seen God. It is God the only Son, who is close to the Father's heart, who has made him known" (John 1:18). This is the same image, that of a little boy curled up against his daddy. Jesus is always attached to, turned toward, and aimed at the Father, and the beloved disciple does the same thing with Jesus, listening to his heart. Now we can understand the expression, "As the Father has sent me, so I send you" (John 20:21).

"Receive the Holy Spirit": now God's nature can enter into us; now we can live on love and forgiveness. "If you forgive the sins of any, they are forgiven them." Now we can have mercy. We assume a great responsibility, having given ourselves to our Lord, to deliver his love to others, because he also says, "If you retain the sins of any, they are retained." If you don't do it, who will? If one who has known God's love doesn't do it, who will be able to do it? In order to give this love, we need to have received it.

There is a wide gulf of difference between the love of one's brother or sister and *agape*, the Greek term that's used principally by St. Paul and by the New Testament to indicate love. There exists both love for humanity, for that which is human—and it should be recognized as such—and *agape*, meaning God's love, that which in mortals is poured out by the Holy Spirit. In fact, love for one's fellow humans will always have to do with justice, whereas God's love has to do with forgiveness, with the capacity to give eternal life, to give the Holy Spirit and to be able to be the Spirit's vehicle.

1 John 4:7 says, "Everyone who loves is born of God." Let's be clear that we can calmly ask others to do works of welcoming and acceptance, works of human mercy, philanthropic works—and may God be blessed when men and women open their hearts to what is good. But the works we are talking about are, notably, both spiritual and corporal when referring to the wholeness of the human person.

We can, in fact, do good things for humanity, starting not from love but from a sense of duty, from the impulse of justice or from our goodwill or from a love that's aesthetic and human, but has no everlastingness. But human justice, for example, doesn't save. It doesn't have the Holy Spirit who re-creates, reviving and reconstituting that which is wrong. Our "penitentiaries," for example, are indeed called places of penance, because in those places one who has done wrong ought to live through a reeducation in order to return to being, instead of a negative element in society, a positive one. Forgive me, but I have yet to see anyone leave prison better than he or she entered it—unless someone has placed their trust in that person, loving them. Yes, this I have seen. But it was not the prison that had done the work of growth and newness in that person. It was the love found, on occasion, through the coinciding of geographical location, and not by the structural characteristic. No jail will ever heal a person. Only love heals people. Jails embitter people. A society that demands justice and punishes has no wise understanding: one who leaves jail will maintain a vindictive character. The true cure is mercy.

With those parameters established, when is it that an act of mercy is a work that makes God present? When it's within God, that's obvious. Humans can therefore do good deeds, generic good that's transient and short-term. But the good that contains more—that carries the invisible within itself, that isn't just skin-deep, that's more than biology—implies spiritual mercy that also enlivens the works of corporal mercy. That good is born out of a relationship with God; it's born out of faith. A sick person can't be healed and at the same time be given hope, given an understanding of the meaning of their suffering in Christ and the hope of his Resurrection, if the works of corporal mercy aren't united with those of spiritual mercy; it's outlandish to divide them.

It's impossible to accomplish the works of our faith by carrying out merely physical acts. We can clothe a naked person and only have covered their body, but to give them the dignity of a child of God, as is done in baptism, can only be done with faith. This doesn't imply any condemnation of human works, but we must see them in their beauty and also in their incompleteness, because they don't carry within them eternity, heaven. Blessed are those who do good on earth, for they will be greeted by the Father, who will know how to reward them. But we are called, having known the love of God, to replenish each and every thing that's of eternity, fulfilling those works starting from our relationship with God.

## BODY AND SPIRIT

At this point we can begin to ask ourselves what the works of spiritual and corporal mercy really are.

Love works according to two coordinates, the body and the spirit, because humans are like that: they're made up of a body and a spirit; they have a biological life and an inner life. The Church says that humans are "the oneness of soul and body" (Vatican II, Pastoral Constitution *Gaudium et Spes*, 14). All that in humans is corporal is also spiritual, and all that's spiritual certainly becomes corporal: these are two aspects of the same reality. If we see the corporal works of mercy, involving "giving the hungry something to eat, giving the thirsty something to drink, clothing the naked, welcoming pilgrims, visiting the sick, visiting those who are in prison, burying the dead"—these are all the works that concern the body: feeding, giving, providing clothing, welcoming, visiting, burying. Concerning a physical reality, these are objective.

The spiritual works of mercy, on the other hand, are "counseling the doubtful, instructing those who are ignorant, admonishing sinners, comforting the afflicted, forgiving offenses, patiently bearing with those who wrong us, praying to God for the living and the dead." Counsel, instruct, admonish, comfort, forgive, bear with, pray for. These are works that touch the other in the reality of their spirit, in their psychological, spiritual part; they stem from the inner reality, concerning the heart, and the challenge is precisely that of caring for the heart.

The spiritual works, more than the corporal ones, have directly to do with faith. The works of corporal mercy, in fact, could also be done factually without faith. The text that explains the corporal works of mercy is Matthew 25:31–40:

"When the Son of Man comes in his glory, and all the angels with him, then he will sit on the throne of his glory. All the nations will be gathered before him, and he will separate people one from another as a shepherd separates the sheep from the goats, and he will put the sheep at his right hand and the goats at the left. Then the king will say to those at his right hand, 'Come, you that are blessed by my Father, inherit the kingdom prepared for you from the foundation of the world; for I was hungry and you gave me food, I was thirsty and you gave me something to drink, I was a stranger and you welcomed me, I was naked and you gave me clothing, I was sick and you took care of me, I was in prison and you visited me.' Then the righteous will answer him, 'Lord, when was it that we saw you hungry and gave you food, or thirsty and gave you something to drink? And when was it that we saw you a stranger and welcomed you, or naked and gave you clothing? And when was it that we saw you sick or in prison and visited you?' And the king will answer them, 'Truly I tell you, just as you did it to one of the least of these who are members of my family, you did it to me.'"

At the beginning of this text it's affirmed that Jesus will gather before himself all the "nations," the "people," the "Gentiles," literally people of all ethnic groups—that is to say, the people who see him for the first time, who haven't had an explicit profession of faith in his name, who don't know they have done something for him or that they have had a relationship with him. The universal judgment will reveal this, when it will be manifest that which is authentic, that which humans have done well. It would therefore seem that there is no need to have explicit faith in Jesus Christ in order to carry out the corporal works of mercy. Mercy comes from God, but humans can do these works on the basis of their humanity.

Indeed, the corporal works of mercy seem more accessible. To clothe the naked seems to be merely a practical problem, and that can appear to be relatively easy, whereas to comfort one who is afflicted would seem to be much more difficult. For the spiritual works of mercy something is needed that's quite different from hands that move. For those works a spiritual character is needed, whereas for the corporal ones the body is sufficient. The corporal works of mercy, as can clearly be seen in Matthew 24, will be required of everyone, and everyone will be judged on whether they have done them or not. Anyone, whether a nonbeliever or a believer, can care for someone; no faith is needed to do that. We can get that far with our humanity. For the spiritual works of mercy, more is needed, it would seem.

But let's pay careful attention to one thing: the challenge isn't to practice the corporal works and practice the spiritual ones. The real challenge is to *join them together*. If they aren't put into practice simultaneously, one is rendered counterfeit in the absence of the other.

Admittedly, it may be true that it's more difficult to comfort one who is afflicted rather than to clothe the naked, and certainly it's true and obvious that comforting one who is afflicted without recognizing that the person needs clothing is grotesque and makes the comfort that's offered seem ridiculous.

It's worth saying: it's not a good strategy to separate them. Pragmatists strip away love from anything eternal; spiritual persons strip it away from reality. There is no heart and there is no heaven in one who despises the spiritual works; there is no body and there is no earth in those who disregard the corporal ones. The Lord Jesus unites in his body heaven and earth, humanity and divinity, body and spirit. And this is our most beautiful adventure: certainly not sectorialization or dismemberment, but the communion of all the dimensions of our existence with the grace of God.

Why are these the spiritual works of mercy, exactly? "Counseling the doubtful, instructing those who are ignorant, admonishing sinners, comforting the afflicted, forgiving offenses, patiently bearing with those who wrong us, praying to God for the living and the dead." In the Scriptures we don't have a single text but rather a collection of texts that take into account an operative wisdom that covers every stage of the various texts.

We have the first document that attests to our list from a master of the faith, Lattanzius (ca. AD 250–325), who did something distinct. This was the time of the great councils—those of Nicaea and Constantinople— a time in which the faith of the church was being crystallized and, while others were inferring the Creed of the church based on theology, Lattanzius wanted to fight against heresies and enunciate the true faith by means of the practices of the Christians: they love like this, they do these things, and from this we understand their faith, we understand what they believe. This is the heart of his discourse.

The Letter of James says, "'You have faith and I have works.' Show me your faith apart from your works, and I by my works will show you my faith" (James 2:18). To be a Christian it isn't enough for someone to tell you who Christ is; you need to see Christ in that person. Christians operate according to the Father, as children of God, and that's how they know how to accomplish the spiritual works. That's how they're capable of a wisdom that bears witness to a different life. They're the eyes, the hands, the understanding of someone who has been born of God. We'll encounter the adventure of how a child of God acts, and therefore how the Father acts. One who doubts receives counsel in a quite precise manner because a gift of counsel has been received from that standing. Such persons know how to teach what truly counts because they have been taught that which only the Father is able to reveal.

Our adventure will be to discover the Christian works that take care of the hearts of others according to a life, a vision of things, an intuition that takes as its starting point the Resurrection of the Lord Jesus and the life that can be received only and uniquely from the sacraments.

St. Paul says something unheard of in 1 Corinthians 2:12–16:

> Now we have received not the spirit of the world, but the Spirit that is from God, so that we may understand the gifts bestowed on us by God. And we speak of these things in words not taught by human wisdom but taught by the Spirit, interpreting spiritual things to those who are spiritual.

> Those who are unspiritual do not receive the gifts of God's Spirit, for they are foolishness to them, and they are unable to understand them because they are spiritually discerned. Those who are spiritual discern all things, and they are themselves subject to no one else's scrutiny.

> "For who has known the mind of the Lord
>    so as to instruct him?"

But we have the mind of Christ.

Your brother-in-law asks you what he should do about a problem that he has at work. What do you tell him? If you have the spirit of the world, out of your own strength you'll talk to him about the triviality of this world, about its craftiness, its dishonesty, its individualism. But if you've received the Spirit of God, you'll know how to help him discover the Providence in that problem; you'll know how to show him the path of love in that tribulation; you'll reveal to him how to find God in that circumstance, how to grow through that apparently cloudy occasion. If you have the mind of Christ.

And what if you don't have it, this mind of Christ? You'll spit out obviousness. You'll see the paralytic and you'll tell him: "You need a doctor here." We're at the level of water that bathes and fire that burns. The truth from nothing to nothing.

Christian people often complain about, in priests, preaching that has no cutting edge. Good feelings and volunteerism. Volunteerism and good feelings, selected at random. Come unto the Lord with songs of boredom.

But really, there is worse. We can arrive at confusion of the type of comforting those who are in error by minimizing the errors, severely admonishing the afflicted, teaching people who wrong us to do exactly what they were doing, and berating those who doubt. This makes for a not-uncommon milkshake of Christian concepts fired by hormonal secretions.

Improvised spiritual direction, unverified counsel, axioms pronounced without preparation but set forth based on confused reminiscences of distant memories from seminary, or from the catechism. Am I exaggerating? Perhaps so. Or perhaps not.

But traveling in the spiritual works of mercy will instead be an adventure in Christian wisdom; it will be a plunge into the "guts" of Christianity, into its nature. A sort of practical treatise on the grace of the Incarnation, on daily enculturation, on how the Holy Spirit inspires us in the various situations we may face.

Therefore, let's begin.

# THE
# SPIRITUAL
# WORKS OF
# MERCY

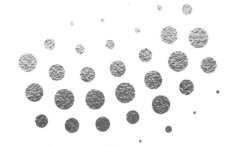

# 1

# COUNSEL THE
# DOUBTFUL

This is the first of the spiritual works of mercy. How shall we navigate, analyzing them one by one? More or less in four phases: First of all, we need to understand the urgency, the distress that we are facing—in our case what is the problem of those who doubt and therefore what mercy they need to find. Second, we will see the imitations of every single work. Accordingly, at last we will understand what they consist of, and, finally, what path to take to arrive at receiving the grace of practicing these acts.

## AN INTERMINABLE SERIES OF CROSSROADS

What problem does a person filled with doubt have? Life is an interminable series of crossroads that place before us options, choices; this is a dramatic aspect of our existence. By choosing this or that path, we sometimes gamble with everything. Some people ruin their lives through their own choices. Others, on the other hand, choose well and save their lives; they leave behind desperation, suffering, or simple bad management.

Each morning we wake up with the need to sift through what is real and authentic, separating what we will do from what we will not do; each thing implies exclusion. The daily choices that can be banal, ordinary, and with little risk, or alternatively, significant, such as being able to compromise a great deal, if not everything. And often we don't even know if a choice is significant or not. Often, we dedicate ourselves outrageously to secondary options, and we distract ourselves from those that are vital by undervaluing them, if not by being slothful, apathetic.

A doubt, in turn, can "stamp out" people to the point of reducing them to a state of inactivity.

There are some people—and this is a newly discovered anthropological fact—who enter into a phase of indecision at around the age of twenty and don't come out of it for a long time. Having been unsuccessful in the phase of identifying their own direction, it's possible to arrive at the age of forty without having made any definitive choice. This is a parking lot from which many don't find the exit, and people in that deadlock don't manage to get married or find their own identity, which is to say that they don't take an unequivocal path. Often, they're conditioned by the surrounding culture that is in fact largely ambiguous.

St. John Paul II, Benedict XVI, and Francis have many times criticized the culture of relativism. Why is this so reviled by the popes? Because it's a culture in which all choices are considered equal, in which freedom is exchanged for the commonplace possibility of choice.

Freedom is much more than that. It requires more. It's the complete possession of ourselves, the beginning of self-determination, the capacity, that is, to stop ourselves, to give ourselves boundaries, to be able to say real, authentic, effective noes and yeses. Those who don't know how to say no to themselves must satisfy all their own wishes. They're not free; they're people in an infantile state, a state of immaturity that they must overcome.

Let's take an example: How does one go about provoking a fit in a child? Take him into a toy store and ask him to choose just one toy. A cruel torture. Having to make a choice, the child will feel, at each hypothetical choice, the choice that will follow that one—namely, the distress of giving up all the other toys; so each choice will correspond to an immense loss. This isn't a good system for bringing up a child.

The way to do it is to guide him in the choice and help him, because this is the age of "discretion," in which he's capable, as it happens, of "discernment." There's a reason for doing that, because a series of such things done with a young child can be considered abusive.

It's sad to think that many parents since the 1970s have put into action this very kind of bloodstained way of educating children: you choose; I'll leave you alone. A child of seven years of age needs to have points of support, not lofty peaks to throw himself up against. A child needs order, schedules. He can't be made to choose when to go to bed or when to eat. It's interesting that these children often, as adolescents, become little soldiers hunting for rules, boxed in by the horror of disorder. You find them at age twenty without a single straight line inside of them, and full of straight lines outside of themselves, in order to stand upright. Then, poor kids, if they find a valid external point of reference, they would break your heart, they're so unhappy. And God save us from seizing that heart. God guard us from putting our handcuffs on those souls that go on instead with help to grow up, to find their structure outside themselves. We need to stay one step behind them. We need to exercise parental integrity, at the risk of disappointing them; that's better, rather than making ourselves indispensable. How many priests have I seen take that path, intoxicated at being a permanent center of gravity: I will have no other priest apart from me. Criminals. God save us and save our young people.

To form a person in the art of choosing requires gentleness, patience, time, and, I repeat, parental integrity. The reality of the choice, doubt, is the dramatic and dizzying condition in which we find ourselves. In order to choose, let's remind ourselves, we necessarily need to lose something. "To lose" in this case means to renounce all that we have not chosen. Getting married, for example, means to choose a spouse and renounce all other possibilities. Consecrating ourselves to God means to choose a path and avoid all the others. Every choice is like that.

What is the consequent problem of doubt? It's the absolutely human condition of not having clarity between one choice and another, not being clear on which is the best path. But at this point two superficial prospects pop up. The principal one is to think that there is a question of an option between good and evil. Perhaps it might be so elementary. If the choice were between good and evil, it would be easy and would follow a scheme. One who must choose between these extremes surely chooses good—that isn't difficult. But it's never so simple. The true choice, in fact, isn't between good and evil but rather between true good and false good. All the options, in serious choices, have at least a semblance of good, and this is what makes life hard.

Those who are filled with doubt, those who have to decide, find themselves at a crossroads, and they don't manage to decide. Why? Even before they arrive at that point, there is a deep problem: life is ambiguous, and it has, at least, a double appearance. Many times, the action of posing the argument on just two options is simplistic.

## THE TEMPTATION OF THE ANCIENT SERPENT

What is the starting point for this reality? The word *doubt*, etymologically, has as its root the word *duo, duality*, the ambiguity of the real. Where does this torture come from?

According to the Scriptures it starts in Genesis 3, from the temptation by the serpent, where another interpretation of the situation appears with respect to the one given by God. Humans have a patently good starting status that at a given moment comes to be perceived in *another* way. God the Creator, the All-Powerful One, the Father, placed humans into a bright reality. But where does temptation insinuate itself? In the interpretation of that reality. While the facts spring from God's all-powerfulness, the interpretation of the same things is subject to one's reading of them, the principles of the interpretation of these things, which can suffer from the ambiguous malice of the devil.

In itself, in the word *devil* the root words *duplicity, rift, splitting, confrontation, antagonism* aren't present by chance.

Sin springs up from this doubt about what is real, and Eve, humanity, falls into that interpretation that carries within it distance from God, first doubting, and then refusing the letter of the reality provided by God, who nonetheless is the Creator, and consequently everything becomes automatically ambiguous.

Satan is the master of this ambiguity. He undermines the sense of what is true and what is beautiful, indicating evil where there is none. Satan doesn't deny that God exists, but he makes us believe that in God, evil is present. Consequently, humans are constrained by that reasoning to determine themselves and their own lives, taking as their starting point the coexistence of all hypotheses, even the worst ones, or rather that of a God who is fundamentally not certain, or not good, or not present, or who doesn't participate. Everything is a possibility.

This way of thinking is what René Descartes, the French philosopher who was the founder of modern rationalism, intended when he affirmed, *Ego cogito, ergo sum, sive existo* (in his *Discours de la méthode,* IV): "I think, therefore I am, meaning that I exist." This way of thinking appears as an abysmal aloneness. There is no help; there is no father or mother; there is no one who can take us by the hand and lead us out of the twilight into the fullness of light: humans must resolve everything on the basis of their own reasoning powers. There is no fundamental relationship in our lives. This is terrifying and sad. And also, because reasoning has devastating limits.

In this twilight, our relationship with God is misguided out of fear, and, nourishing the doubt of the very ambiguity of their Creator, humans consequently lose the capacity of "seeing" things, the facts, in their authentic connotation.

The body, in the account in Genesis, which at first was a reality lived with simplicity, in one stroke became shameful because physicality can now be interpreted either as a simple personal reality or as an instrument of power, of attraction, of exploitation and all that flows from it. Humans must then cover their bodies, because they feel themselves to be objects of an ambiguous gaze. Work, which at first was blessed, becomes cursed, losing its essence as service, of livelihood, of provision, to become the source of revenue or self-affirmation, losing its aspect of brotherhood and sisterhood. At this rate, everything becomes the object of an obscure interpretation, misguided, undermining identity, making all things into merely *things*.

Then there appears, in the extraordinary text in Genesis, a consequent reality of confusion, in which the married partners are no longer mutually dependent upon one another but are out of synch, rivals; and now all of the ambiguous reality and interpreted evil make themselves present. Things, in the darkness, bear the echo of good but also that of evil subject to a risk, that of being read badly and of being used badly. Everything becomes indefinable.

So it happens that also in the most terrible depravity, there is always the memory of something good and, also in the highest good, there is the fear of a latent evil. We are in the absurd reality of having to find something justifiable in evil and something valid in good, but up to a certain point, in which there remains nonetheless something suspect. Let's think, for example, about how justice can wind up justifying violence.

This ambiguity seems to be in things, but in reality, it's in the heart—because it's the heart itself that welcomes or refuses that reading marked by goodwill that God gives us. Through this it's worth the trouble to begin to ask ourselves whether the solution for doubt is outside ourselves. Humans, when they hear that voice that says, in a nutshell, that God doesn't love them, have lost their security, their confidence, their trust. They think that God has become angry with them, and they must, in the end, be worthy of his love. And so it is with Adam and Eve. Evil uses this temptation by putting us in the condition of reading reality from a double, triple, or even more, a multiple point of view.

This ambiguity is one of human blindness, of over-reading, a projection of our own interior ambiguity. Humans find themselves in a reality that's subject to this incomplete reading. There is always something that could be the opposite of what it appears to be. We think that something can be good, whereas it's bad, or vice versa. How do we resolve this problem?

Let's be clear: doubts are of various types. There are things that we really don't know. And we doubt them until we receive objective facts. Here the problem is, rather, that of making doubts come. Indeed, another is not to have clarified all the terms of a question—which is a condition of the simple absence of facts. Another is to hit the ground running when we don't yet have all the elements—and this is pride, conceit, arrogance. Another is to remain at the crossroads among different possibilities of reading the choices, and this is what we have been dealing with up till now.

The first case, that of the lack of necessary information, is forgivable. We don't compromise our souls for that. Mistakes made out of a lack of facts don't soil the heart; they make us suffer in practice, but not existentially. But it's easy to fall into the second case, that in which nothing is put on the table for discussion, we don't turn to seeing whether everything has been examined, we don't consider with humility whether we are not undervaluing or overvaluing something. Those mistakes hurt us. And also because they cancel out the mercy of others, making us incapable of listening, causing us to endure advice as an invasion, as making us into babies, whereas it's we who are pigheadedly attached to a synthesis that is at the very least hasty.

But when confronted with a person who is really in doubt, what are the wrong strategies? This is the important question: What are the imitations of that work? This is something we've already mentioned;

let's see about crystallizing it better. The temptation of those who counsel doubtful people rotates around two opposing polarities.

Let's begin with the lesser one: the tendency toward rationalism and hyper-analysis, done while setting about to sort through the facts, looking for the "objective" solution, Sherlock Holmes-style, as if there exist sicknesses and not sick people, facts and not people who do things and live through things. And this leads in a flash to a schematic approach: you set me onto one of your problems, and I look for the schema, the pattern in which to put you, sticking you into a pigeon hole without really listening to you. This is "professional" advice. The person in a state of doubt is placed, by hammer blows, into the list of things that we already know. Nonetheless, nothing at all is ever repeated. Things don't happen twice, as C. S. Lewis says.[1]

What are we referring to? Superficiality, at times exhibitionism of supposed wisdom, but nonetheless the schematic approach.

But the other pole is the worst: paternalism. I remember a meeting of priests in which the one who was presiding asked the question, "What should one of the faithful find in a spiritual father?" One of those present answered, "A clear indication about what God's will is; he should know how to tell this with certainty to the one who asks him." I've never forgotten the chill and the outrage that this affirmation provoked in me. I reacted badly, saying out loud that I was getting out of that crowd of paternalistic men. The one who was presiding, who respected me, asked me to explain myself. I don't know if I was understood by those brethren, but I said that a good father isn't the one who solves his children's problems, but the one who teaches his children to solve their problems.

How many times have I had to repeat that sentence. How many spiritual dictators (rather than spiritual *directors*) have I met, lay and priests, who turn people into children in the name of obedience, leaving them in a juvenile condition by means of an ill-advised axiom: solving

---

1  C. S. Lewis, *The Chronicles of Narnia* (Italian version—Milan: Mondadori, 2005), 567.

the problem is more important than causing the person to grow. And the next time, what will that brother or sister do? They will have to turn back to me to ask me what to do, because I haven't helped them grow in the problem, but rather I've given them the solution. I repeat: the solution becomes more important than my sister or brother.

In some cases it isn't true that we have to resolve a doubt, but rather that we need to take a walk through our own hearts. And what do we find? The simple answer? No. It's as if I went to see a film and someone told me the ending after five minutes. Great, thanks, and now what do I see the film doing for me? The pleasure was entirely in getting there by degrees. . . .

The pleasure of an equation in tenth grade, when I was in high school, was in succeeding at designing the parabola of the equation. As if it were better to be carried in a cable car to the top of a mountain rather than to climb it. I understand laziness, but that's something entirely different! Then the mountain is mine, and in my muscles, I've fought for it, I've learned so many things, I have so much to remember and so much to share.

No! Instead it's a burden, at the top, to have been hauled up and set there.

A doubt is a path of growth, a challenge; good heavens, it's an adventure.

What is to be done with this child? Should I enter seminary? Do I leave behind this job? What truly counts? Tell me what to say to this rambunctious young man. I tell you, and then? I tell you that he has a vocation, and then? I tell you: this isn't the job you are suited for. And then? How do you manage the critical situation that for sure will come later? If you don't own the decision, the renunciation that's involved, the necessary maturation, you'll do things that will look like a Lego brick. Obtuse. Out of place.

41

## THE CERTAINTIES OF THE DOUBTFUL

Our work of mercy is precisely to counsel those who doubt, but what does it mean to give counsel? *Consulere*, in Latin, means "to sit alongside someone," "to be next to him or her." What does that mean, and how can we work on that point? One who doubts is worn out by the ambiguity of what is real and isn't able to distinguish between what is true good and what is false good.

If we look in the Gospels, Jesus doesn't resolve doubts by unraveling them, setting forth the questions in an articulate and critical manner, as so many of us Westerners like so much to do. Rather, he does everything in a completely different way, radical and Semitic, that seems a bit disappointing to our desire to understand everything. We find this attitude throughout the Old Testament, which doesn't demonstrate the existence of God; it starts from his existence, stars it, affirms something with certainty. It doesn't demonstrate the existence of the evil one; it shows him in action. It doesn't talk about human weakness by seeking to articulate a discourse, explaining it, justifying it, but rather it simply sets it forth as real. We think we're resolving doubts by analyzing them—that seems obvious, and certainly, doubts need to be heard; this is a sign of maturity—but the solution for doubt, in fact, isn't in doubt: we don't realize this, and we almost never remember it.

St. John Paul II, in the vigil with young people at World Youth Day in Toronto in 2002, said, *Is it right to be content with provisional answers to the ultimate questions, and to abandon life to the impulses of instinct, to short-lived sensations or passing fads?*[2] This whole marvelous speech ended in a splendid exhortation, improvised on the spot, not to leverage doubts but rather certainties, not to rely on what is ambiguous but on what is sharp and clear.

This seems obvious, but this is actually what we don't do. So how can this be done, and where do we start? When we are faced with a doubt, we need to remove ambiguity from reality. What is the way to

2   Pope John Paul II, address at the evening vigil with young people, 17th World Youth Day, Toronto, Canada, Downsview Park, Saturday, July 27, 2002.

put things right? We must start from what is certain, from a reference point. So, do those who give the solution do well? I am not saying that, but rather something quite different. We need to start from certainties, but not from the certainties of the one consulted, but rather from those who doubt. And this implies making doubters talk, getting to know them, letting the crux of their doubts come out.

Jesus, in John 11:21–27, carries on a developing dialogue with Martha:

> Martha said to Jesus, "Lord, if you had been here, my brother would not have died. But even now I know that God will give you whatever you ask of him." Jesus said to her, "Your brother will rise again." Martha said to him, "I know that he will rise again in the resurrection on the last day." Jesus said to her, "I am the resurrection and the life. Those who believe in me, even though they die, will live, and everyone who lives and believes in me will never die. Do you believe this?" She said to him, "Yes, Lord, I believe that you are the Messiah, the Son of God, the one coming into the world."

Martha spoke first, and, in her anguish, in her thinly disguised reprimand, expresses something constructive, proactive. Jesus starts from what is a certainty for her, from the certainty of Jesus's extraordinary relationship with the God of Israel, and then he leverages her faith in the resurrection of the dead, and therefore he triangulates on her experience, her faith that he really is the Messiah. At that point Martha is ready to cross the threshold of a true and proper act of faith. If the preceding points are put together, and if she believes that Christ is the Son of God, then she can "open herself up" to believing in the resurrection of her brother—she is wide open to it. Mary speaks, and then Martha, and she—not Mary—has the stone rolled away from the tomb of her brother, Lazarus. And what happens, happens. We would need to read this text more in depth, though this isn't the right time for that. But this is an example of removing ambiguity.

So how can we go about escaping this ambiguous system? St. Paul, in 2 Corinthians 1:17–20, writes:

> Was I vacillating when I wanted to do this? Do I make my plans according to ordinary human standards, ready to say "Yes, yes" and "No, no" at the same time? As surely as God is faithful, our word to you has not been "Yes and No." For the Son of God, Jesus Christ, whom we proclaimed among you, Silvanus and Timothy and I, was not "Yes and No"; but in him it is always "Yes." For in him every one of God's promises is a "Yes." For this reason it is through him that we say the "Amen," to the glory of God.

The point of strength is to start from "yeses," from certainties, and to announce things sharply and clearly and with simplicity. Our doubts are anchored in the ancient doubt prompted by the serpent. In that "no," the doubt that in God there may be present both love and not-love, that reality may be a salvation story but also not. The ancient hymn the *Te Deum* says, *In te, Dómine, sperávi, non confúndar in aetérnum*: "Our hope is in you; throughout eternity we shall not be in confusion."

The Gospel is the announcement of a "yes," which is the pivotal and central point for reading all the rest of life. If we think that life bubbles up from an ambiguous spring and not from the hands of Providence, we find ourselves facing life with our hands raised in self-defense, and doubts torture us. We exit from this by thinking about the "yes" that God is for us, in our hearts holding on to the fact God can't stop loving us.

It should be noted that Jesus becomes angry when it's attributed to him that he casts out demons in the name of evil (Matt. 12:22–32). He doesn't accept this and speaks of sin against the Holy Spirit, where ambiguity is specifically attributed to God. That ambiguity doesn't exist! God is only love (1 John 4:8). This is the point from which we can start to help one who doubts. It isn't reason, as a matter of fact, that resolves doubts, but love. Love gives much deeper principles than reason, without excluding it, without contradicting it. It uses reason and goes beyond it. Love is reasonable, and at the same time it's even wiser. To counsel one who doubts, we need love; we need to listen. It isn't a matter only and simply of unraveling what the doubting person must discover.

The choices are made, indeed, in first person singular. This adult status of choices remains obligatory, but counseling one who must choose requires that we make ourselves the echo of God's "yes," the motherly support of his love, which comes before everything, in order to engender support of things that are certain.

An existential dilemma isn't read from the depths of confusion but from the heights of certainty of the love of God. We will return to this, but it's urgent to see what the traits are of those who practice mercy in giving counsel.

It's true that the first characteristic of good counselors is that they understand the things being said to them, that they're perceived to be understanding, listening. This helps considerably because to unpack our statements in front of someone, to tell our own doubts, to explain what questions we have, very often is already the beginning of resolving our problems.

But a good counselor's listening has a quite specific quality. The good counselor doesn't start from searching for answers but from asking questions. The challenge is to find the question that indicates things in the proper perspective. Not to challenge what is seen but rather the point of view, which can be distorted by so many elements— and one doesn't see the essence of things because there is something turned upside down; there is deception or misconception somewhere. If things begin to be put into order, then it's possible also to understand the specific burdens of things. Almost always an erroneous question is where things get off. It's necessary to sniff it out, but the one who doubts is the one to ferret it out, not the counselor. Certainly, from the outside this is easier, but this has to be done at the pace of the one who doubts, otherwise along the way we will leave people buried alive, people who then will undermine the clarity of the discernment.

To find the erroneous question counselors need to analyze the starting point, the position, the center of gravity from which they observe the situation. This is the problem of doubt. The evil one definitely works by putting us in the wrong place to see things. The Greek word *eidolon*, from the verb "to see," means "idol," but it has an etymological meaning of "perspective," "vision," "way of seeing." Where does perspective come from? Why do we not manage to make up our minds? We can rationalize a lot, but the perspective with which we look at reality isn't normally rational but rather irrational; it doesn't reside in reasons but rather in motives. Therefore, we need a healthy detachment that helps us turn toward seeing things in the correct perspective.

Psalm 49:21 says, "Mortals cannot abide in their pomp; they are like the animals that perish." Let's remember that the spiritual works of mercy are closely related to the seven gifts of the Holy Spirit, this one more than all the others.

Among the seven gifts of the Holy Spirit is the gift of counsel, the capacity to choose according to one's light. What do we need in order to choose according to the Holy Spirit? St. Philip Neri, in the principal prayers of the visit of the Seven Churches, with a simple and remarkable synthesis, puts the gifts of the Holy Spirit in opposition to the capital sins, and the one that opposes the capacity to choose and advise, surprisingly, is greed. You think about it and it seems obvious: Who and what doesn't manage to proceed to a choice? One who doesn't manage to separate themselves from things. We saw this abundantly in the first part: every choice implies a loss. Therefore, what is needed is detachment, freedom from things.

Misers are those who throw nothing away. They hang on to everything, dwelling in the anxiety that doesn't allow them to let go of anything. In the most difficult discernments, indeed, the road to a decision often passes through serious almsgiving. In almsgiving, when it isn't mediocre, when it's done "at the cost of blood," seriously touching our possessions, we experience a paschal sense of loss followed by joy. The product of giving alms is a sense of liberation, and at the same time also of the possession of ourselves. It's understood that money isn't in command, but rather we are in command; the heart has won the victory over things. When we go back to examine the decision that, in a state of doubt, we were not capable of undertaking, we discover that we have gained freedom, that we are no longer afraid of losing something because we have had the experience that when we "lose" nothing happens, that being attached to things prevents us from choosing freely.

The gift of counsel, which is opposed to avarice, is what we need in order to overcome the ambiguity of our lives. We need an inner satellite reference point, a place from which the sun rises, from the east, from a point of orientation; we need parameters. To find the parameters of choices, we need to start from a determination—which seems obvious but it isn't—that's inherent in our search: to find the parameter I need to start from the assertion that a parameter exists. That is to say, that truth exists.

In the reality of our lives there exists something objective, which is called truth. If I neglect myself, for example, I am worse off—this is true; it's simply reality. If I don't take care of my relationships with others, I am in a bad way. If I don't govern my life and my impulses, I destroy myself. In the summer the weather is hotter than in winter. In our hemisphere, that's clear. Truth exists, and the very fact that we are searching for it, St. Augustine affirms, attests to the fact that it exists:

> If what I am telling you is not clear to you, and you doubt that it is true, take care at least whether you are doubting your doubting it. And if you are certain you are doubting, look for the motive by which you are certain. . . . Whoever understands that they are doubting, understands the truth, and what it understands is certain; therefore, they are certain of the truth. This means that whoever doubts the existence of truth has within themselves the truth, by which they cannot doubt it. But what is true is uniquely so through the truth. For this reason, they must not

doubt the truth that they have doubted for some kind of reason. (Augustine, *On True Religion*, 39.73)

Remain, if you can, in the initial clarity of this rapid flash of lightning that dazzles you, when it calls itself Truth. (Augustine, *The Trinity*, 8.2)

This is one of our requirements, and we do better if we keep that in mind.

The truth exists. We can't approach it in a simplistic, coarse manner, but it exists. Our journey is from ambiguity to certainty. And where does certainty come from? From the confidence and trust that, through experience, parental esteem grows. And what are we to do with the ambiguous parents of today? Where do we find certainty? Let's look at a liturgical case.

When priests are ordained—as is the case when deacons are ordained—the one who presents the candidate says, "Reverend Father, Holy Mother Church asks that these brothers be admitted to the order of the priesthood." The bishop replies, "Are you certain that they are worthy of this?" He doesn't ask them if they're worthy, but the one who, in the name of the Church, is presenting them. He doesn't ask exactly if they're worthy, but whether the one who is presenting them has certainty on this subject: "Are you certain of this?" This question is addressed directly to that person, who is often the rector of the seminary, and this person replies in the first person singular, in front of the candidates: "From the information gathered among the Christian people and according to the judgment provided by those who have looked after their formation, I can attest that they're worthy of this."

The candidates must hear this: "Yes, you are suited to this; you can do it. We are admitting you to the order of the diaconate or the priesthood because we have a certainty about you; you are worthy of this charge and of this grace." And the bishop responds in return: "With the help of God and of Jesus Christ our Savior; we choose these sons for the order of the priesthood." The implications of this curious dialogue are many, and are deep, but we note the total passivity of the candidates. They must receive many things that day, but in this passage, they receive the public confirmation of a certainty: someone thinks that you can do this, and this "someone" is the Church community. They will need this certainty a thousand times, to have an impact on what is genuine and true, and to take possession of the gifts that will serve them to build the Church.

If we don't receive confidence and trust, we will not have confidence and trust; if we don't have someone who tells us that we can make it, we won't make it. This confidence and trust come from the parent because, let's repeat, it grows from parental confidence and trust. Some parents shake their heads and say, "You can't make it." The consequence is that the children have had no confidence, no trust. If instead a parent says to a child, "Come on, you'll see that you can do it," the consequence is the trust that he or she will be able to do it, and their own qualities will come out. They will become capable of bringing out the best in themselves.

Humans are the bearers of so much beauty; their lives are so precious in the sight of God. This confidence, this trust, is the fundamental point; to live well it's necessary to have it. How many times have I set a young person in front of a crucifix and told him or her: "Now you stay here, and we will talk again only when God tells you who you are according to him. When God has told you this, we will take up the process of discernment again." The young person turns after a little while, and I ask them: "What did he tell you?" And they answer, "That he loves me, that he was ready to die for me, that I am important."

It's here that we need to place our orientation: in the fact that the Lord, even when we may have made mistakes, doesn't abandon us. He continues to have confidence in us; he continues to pronounce his "yes" for us. The greatest number of mistakes, especially in young people, come from having so little care for themselves. If these things are seen from God's perspective, from his tenderness, from his mercy, everything changes. Our lives are not a mistake; they don't have an ambiguous nature, but they carry within themselves the objective realities, the certainties that we must be conscious of and from which we must not allow ourselves to run away. The fight is aimed at defending this awareness, that of being loved, of possessing in ourselves that beauty and fullness that makes life itself. So, in order to counsel the doubtful, we need first of all to have them start from the certainty of God's love.

To counsel the doubtful implies, as we have seen, causing them to recenter themselves on the deepest of certainties. This is going to be affirmed, embodied, surrendered. This is the strength of the counselor. Counselors are not those who elaborate facts; they're witnesses, they have experience with the rock that resists wind and tide, they have plumbed to the depths of life, to its roots. No, there is no doubt: God loves you. This isn't just a worn-out saying; what I am telling you resides in my flesh, in my heart, in my innermost being, in my ministry or in my marriage, in my life. But if this is formulated as a question, it has a very different import. The ball must remain in the court of the one whose doubt is growing. "Could it be that God has decided to forget you?" A question that I've so often had fun asking is this: "What do you say? Does God love you or me more?" Or, "Does he love you more, or me, or St. Francis?" When people recognize that they're God's offspring, when they open their hearts to his tenderness, so many things untangle. True doubt is always like that; ultimately, I've never encountered any other.

At this point counselors can leverage the pivot points of life, the essential things. For discernment we need to start from the "yeses" that we have already received. How do we recognize them? What is good is simple and linear, in contrast with evil, which is tortuous and contradictory. Evil, in order to be carried out, upon a close look always has to be justified. The good carries with it its own self-evidence in our hearts. When true good touches our hearts, there aren't myriad ways to snarl things up; in our souls there springs up a light that can't be doubted.

Psalm 51:5–6 says, "Indeed, I was born guilty, a sinner when my mother conceived me. You desire truth in the inward being; therefore teach me wisdom in my secret heart." Our best ally is our heart; it's there that we know that our life is beautiful. The wisdom that the psalm talks about affirms that even though we were born poor sinners, we were not born by chance; this awareness is that which saves those who doubt, showing them the clearness of truth. Clarity and simplicity start out from the linchpin of things that are sharp and clear. At this point it seems useful to make a list of certain things in our own lives, things that should not be put into discussion. Normally, as we follow this path, doubts melt away, dwindle, and are less distressing. Now it's a matter of arriving at unambiguous things that are already present within us. These are gifts of God, done in our lives. We need to leverage these things.

## THE PATH OF THE COUNSELOR

And how are we going to carry out this work of mercy? And where are these counselors who radiate such light? Through which door will they enter? What path have they taken? That of experience with the love of God and with being poor in spirit, with detachment, just as with that of freedom and of having become familiar with their own deceitfulness and of having learned to come to terms with it.

I know there are courses in spiritual direction, but how can we go about turning fatherhood and motherhood into a technique? Do we need to know how to speak? Yes, in part, but above all we need to know how to keep silent. Otherwise we can't have a minimum of pedagogy, of strategy; the one vomits out quickly what he or she sees, and the other doesn't grow. What is needed is firmness and gentleness in the same mouthful. And rootedness in the fatherhood and motherhood of God. And no haste to offer solutions; a counselor isn't a skeet shooter.

51

Let's help ourselves, in order to find the path of the counselor, by a splendid text of Blaise Pascal—which makes me look bad as well:

> We need to know how to doubt when necessary, affirm when it is necessary, submit when it is necessary. One who does not behave in this way does not understand the strength of reason There are people who mistakenly fight against these three principles, either affirming that everything is certain, because they do not aim at a demonstration, or they doubt everything because they do not know whom to submit to. Or they submit to everything because they do not know when they ought to use judgment.[3]

Doubt—affirm—submit.

There's a time in which it's good to doubt; doubt is necessary in order to change position, perspective. This requires humility so as not to take our opinions as absolute, remembering that I'm always a work in progress. The daily bread of one who wants to give counsel is the art of knowing our own blunders.

There's no way around it: unfortunately, we can't escape some expressions in Psalm 119, of this type (vv. 71, 75–76):

> It is good for me that I was humbled,
>     so that I might learn your statutes.
> I know, O LORD, that your judgments are right,
>     and that in faithfulness you have humbled me.
> Let your steadfast love become my comfort
>     according to your promise to your servant.

How much does life have to slap me around for me to begin to discover my deceitfulness, my trickery? I ought to know to doubt what I think. A psychologist friend of mine says that mental health is the dis-connection from our own egos. How true this is! Good counselors know how not to take themselves too seriously. They remember how they themselves have turned matters into absolutes; they come to terms

3  Blaise Pascal, *Thoughts: Submission*, 268.

with their own mistakes in reading. And hence they're cautious and good-natured when faced with how others turn matters into absolutes.

The primary road to the training of counselors is to remember their own mixed mistakes in making themselves available to discover mistakes in others. This is a turn of phrase to say: humility. Those who receive as gifts the experience of humiliation and the grace of their own limits.

Good counselors are not those who are strong, but rather they are those who are weak persons who have accepted their own weakness.

So, they deal with inner small stuff.

Then there is certainty, by which some things should not be placed into discussion—simple things, those that seem obvious, knowing the things that are certain in our lives, places toward which to point our compass. We need to be clear about where good arises in our hearts. We need to quench our thirst deeply in that sweet spring. We need to have recorded the good rules of our own happiness. A couple, for example, as soon as they're engaged, ought always to have the ten commandments of things that do their relationship good, and from the care and constancy of these good things there will arise parents who are wise, peaceful, calm, and cheerful.

To grow in the ability to give counsel, counselors need to be constant in healthy living. What does a counselor who drinks too much have to offer? Prayer, good habits, a life of sharing, the exercise of forthrightness and freedom from things: such a person has a clear setting in which to listen. Those who are involved with themselves end up projecting themselves, because they're distressed.

I clean my glasses in order to see better. If I stop my ears and cover my eyes, what am I supposed to understand?

Those who dedicate themselves to spiritual direction need calm and not a show of hyper-efficiency. They don't need to be know-it-all psychologists-anthropologists-sociologists, but they need seriously to be intimately familiar with the Father, to be sons and daughters of the Son, and to rest in the Spirit and to speak from that perspective.

And, last, they're trained in submitting to that certainty; that is, they grow little by little by means of obedience as sons and daughters, surrendering themselves. Because there is no better father than one who knows how to be a son, no better mother than one who knows how to be a daughter. Then they will become ready in the art of giving counsel when they have undertaken the path of the disciples, that of obedience. This isn't a heroic act—please, let's act a bit less like victims. Obedience to God is the simple truth of things, not a just-in-case. It isn't because I am so good that I obey. Rather, I am too dumb not to obey.

Obedience to God is a question of the meaning or flow of things, of reality. It's a measure of practice—it isn't only spiritual. Things are what they are.

The first discernment is to remember how much we need God and his mercy.

Indeed.

# 2

# INSTRUCT THE IGNORANT

The second spiritual work of mercy helps another human misery: ignorance. What type of misery is it? What urgency can it have?

Every biological life has its finality, its own constitution, an identity. Animals have their instinct: felines are predators, mice are rodents, dogs are trackers. Every species has its own instinct, its own "flair." And humans?

The human attitude, on the other hand, is quite different. Humans possess intellect, reason, and they weigh, analyze reality, comprehend. Can they live without that? Among the various prerogatives of bipeds is the torture to which every parent is put through for a period of time: the "why?" phase. A child can become a broken record that at every affirmation he or she counters with a "why?" I've seen parents ground down by this phase. . . .

For a child this is the healthy exploration of life, the discovery of the mechanism of the real, the rewarding and fulfilling analysis of the links among things.

But for an adult it's quite another story. Not to understand, for humans, is a condition of particular suffering, and "whys" torture us.

It's no small thing that on the cross Jesus cried out, "*My God, my God, why have you forsaken me?*" (Matt. 27:46; Mk. 15:34). The "why" is the center of Christ's pain. And it concerns the expression of the greatest human anguish, that of being alone, abandoned. This fear materializes from the very first instant of life, as the baby exits from the mother's womb. In that moment safety and security are lost, and the child enters into the question, "What's happening to me?" The drama of birth marks us inwardly, revealing a traumatic aspect that affects all of life, by which, consequently, we look for answers to questions such as, "Why was I born? Why am I in this world? Who am I? What am I supposed to do?" These are questions that reveal how humans need information providing meaning and purpose.

Let's repeat: we are not dealing with something superfluous, but with something that's necessary.

Often, we suffer more by the lack of meaning and purpose of painful things, than by the pain that has provoked them.

To incorporate information is inscribed in humans. Some older people look at a vast amount of news every day, and they are actually able to recognize and point out the comparisons among the various editions: "This one said that," perhaps watching the same news service several times. What is an older person expressing through this compulsion for information? It's their need to be up on life, to be current. To know what is happening, not to be cut off.

So many people follow televised political debates even late at night, and they ask themselves how they can manage to wake up and go to work the next day. And then there is the vast sea of the Internet with all its payload of virtual news. And there is an infinite waste of time chasing the most idiotic information.

Behind all this is the desire to know, to receive facts, to understand, which, let's repeat, isn't an optional but rather a necessary activity. We can't make it without that. Humans, using information, using what we know, decide what we are.

Conscious of this human condition, dictatorships lean toward being occupied with information. Indeed, when one wishes to govern a reality, one needs to manipulate the news. It's sufficient to furnish misleading information to a society to influence its life.

Antonio Gramsci, an Italian Marxist, talked explicitly about a "cultural hegemony" that's capable of manipulating the conscience, explaining that the true revolution is actually cultural, not in doing, but in making people think. Gramsci affirmed in one writing,

> There is no human activity from which it is possible to exclude all intellectual intervention. *Homo faber* [humans controlling their fate and their environment through tools] cannot be separated from *homo sapiens* [humans controlling their fate and their environment through knowledge]. Every human, in the end, outside of their occupation explaining some kind of intellectual activity, is, in other words, a "philosopher," an artist, a person of taste, participating in an understanding of the world. Humans have a deliberate line of moral conduct, and therefore they contribute to sustain or to modify an understanding of the world—in other words, to inspire new ways of thinking.[4]

It's a given that many history books used in teaching were written by people of a certain political orientation, capable of furnishing information that if not doctored, is nevertheless enhanced. To accomplish this, it's possible to develop the objective facts of some historical moments. This is the case with the Middle Ages or of the Risorgimento or otherwise, the reading of which could appear quite different from how it was told. I have no desire to provoke arguments, nor to defend the indefensible, but the reality of the questions is often different, and it has been told with an undeniable interpretive orientation. And this has produced a culture that's chock full of clichés, of artfully provoked opposition or agreement.

In the marvelous but disturbing book *1984*, an anti-utopian novel, George Orwell hypothesizes a type of dictatorship that was carried out in a way that was vaguely similar to the Soviet Union and other places: an observer called Big Brother controls the entire lives of humans and is the image of a malignant dictatorship that invades every corner of human existence. The big "eye" possesses a Ministry of Truth that's in

4   Antonio Gramsci, *Quaderni dal carcere (Notebooks from Jail)*, 1523.

a position to furnish information that's manipulated in a way so as to subdue humanity and dominate it:

> The Ministry of Truth—Minitrue, in Newspeak—was startlingly different from any other object in sight. It was an enormous pyramidal structure of glittering white concrete, soaring up, terrace after terrace, 300 metres into the air. From where Winston stood it was just possible to read, picked out on its white face in elegant lettering, the three slogans of the Party:
> WAR IS PEACE
> FREEDOM IS SLAVERY
> IGNORANCE IS STRENGTH[5]

In the phenomenon of the child soldier we can see the power of conditioning, the result of indoctrination that, despite being hardly refined, is nonetheless effective.

Years ago, an American military man was talking to me quite comfortably about his assignment in psychological warfare. I was flabbergasted by how candidly he talked about manipulation of information, which for him was an instrument like any other.

Right. Except, the instruments of the military are called weapons. . . .

## THE NEED TO KNOW

Humans are hungry for meaning and therefore for facts, and as a consequence they can be manipulated. Things can be reversed in perspective; all that's needed is to rearrange the parameters a bit. And they find themselves full of facts, but ignorant. And without understanding. Ignorance all the way.

Everybody instructs the ignorant. We need to see if this is a work of mercy. The chaplain of an enormous media company did that for five years. I've often asked journalists if they were sure that this was salvation for them. They thought I was joking, but I was serious, seeing that some of them—charitably speaking, some, not all—were doing their jobs, nicely following in the tracks of their first colleague. Who am I talking about?

---

5   George Orwell, *1984*, chap. 1, p. 6.

The first misleading informer, in fact, appears in our well-known text from Genesis 3, in which the serpent, who dispenses information with sly cunning, which in reality is the twisted bearer of darkness, in order to refute the wisdom of Eve and make her ignorant under the impression of becoming wise, asks: *Did God say, 'You shall not eat from any tree in the garden?'*[6] This is precisely the question of a journalist—loaded, embarrassing—to which the best answer is "No comment," though the Bible doesn't yet know that term. Eve takes the bait, as happens when confronted with a question that takes for granted something shady that must be justified. But the serpent, once he has embroiled Eve in his discourse, launches his attack (Gen. 3:4–5): But the serpent said to the woman, *"You will not die; for God knows that when you eat of it your eyes will be opened, and you will be like God, knowing good and evil."*

This affirmation contains cunning subtlety; it can't be taken lightly. The serpent furnishes altered information that wants to touch on something quite precise, Eve's memory, in which experience was deposited, and therefore on the memory of her relationship with God.

The essential structure of human consciousness, indeed, is our memory, and it's structured on what we have in our hearts: the Italian *ricordo*—I remember—is based on *cor, cordis* in Latin: the heart. Memories, deposited in the heart, are linked to the affective dimension, not the objective one, and they're able to delineate the human person and condition our choices and our approach to life.

6  Genesis 3:1. To tell the truth, the modern translation is imprecise. Literally, the Hebrew of the text plays on an ambiguity that even in English it is possible to trigger. The text could be: "Is it true that God said: you shall not eat of all the trees in the garden?" There are various pitfalls, but one is that of playing on "not all the trees." There are two meanings present: (1) You shall not eat of any tree—totally forbidding eating from trees. (2) You shall not eat from *all* of the trees—partially forbidding, meaning there are some trees from which you shall not eat. In English it is possible to play on this ambiguity: "You may not read all books" can be understood as (1) you may not read any book at all; (2) you may not read all books. Therefore, by means of logic, the serpent doesn't actually say something false, because it is true that Eve may not eat from all trees. But the play between absolute and partial forbidding is set in motion. Eve replies as if she must justify an absolute prohibition. And so she entered into the operating system of the serpent.

The first journalist, the serpent, asked for comment on a fact and then manipulated that information so as to place poppycock into the human heart. This was his objective. He doesn't stuff the fruit into her mouth; Eve takes it herself. All he had to do was trigger her.

Often underneath existential anguish and distress and the errors that derive from it, there is a lie. People become trapped because they construct themselves on a tall tale, founding their lives on bad information, a distortion, an erroneous interpretation of reality. There is a black pit behind our egoism, behind our rapacity, a nucleus of falsehood that in some way has made us alone and despairing.

Then we understand how urgent it is to instruct and reexamine reality starting from that essential, precious parameter that is the parenthood of God. Only in this way does it become possible to contrast the false measures of judgment that attack our existence.

But what has been remarked here is what we always have as teachers, whether we know it or not. Let's never, ever improvise. Learning is at the base of our wisdom, and all who are born always start as a blank page on which someone writes. We are written—penned—interiorly by the one who has taught us to live.

Who? Just about everyone. Parents teach the hearts of their children to follow a straight path, by means of their actions, their replies, their silences, their pauses, their presence, their haste. Was this all mercy? And then there are one's playmates, the media, one's educators—may I stop this list?

I know well that when I am to announce the Gospel—and by the way, Jesus was also a bit of a journalist; he announced the kingdom of heaven; it's better to say it, or else the authorities will prosecute me—the information I supply must counteract an overwhelming amount of deformed and contrary teaching. My only strength is that what I say is greater than me, surpasses me enormously, but it also surpasses all that the young people who listen to me know already. It has a simple strength of its own, soap and water, without anything optional. It comes from the love of the Father who is in heaven. It knows the heart and is able to conquer because it doesn't impose, but only propose. It's respect, it's esteem for the one who listens, it knows about patience, and it encourages and heals. It doesn't leverage fear, but instead it leverages the depth of things and brings them back to their dignity. And so much more.

## THE EDIFICATION OF THE OTHER

What does it mean to instruct? To give a simple etymology of *instruct* we can start from its relationship with the word *construct*, and refer to the edification of the other. *Insegnare* in Italian—meaning "teach" or "instruct"—is "to write within," "to imprint," "to place into a hollow" in the heart of the other. The antithesis, on the other hand, is "ignore," in the sense of "not to know," which indicates a gnosis—a knowing—preceded by a prefix that indicates taking away something: "not to know."

Instruct the ignorant. It's easy to understand the gravity of this work, but it's necessary to focus our attention on the dramatic deficiency of today: Christian formation. Those who set about to do some Christian act sooner or later discover their lack of upbringing and formation. In order to carry out to the fullest a Christian approach, we must have been brought up to do it, to have a consciousness of how much it's doing, the perception of whether how much we do is inherited and has little to do with faith, and that we save ourselves from falling into actions that are banal, mediocre, having no regard to any kind of eternal nature.

The problem is to form and educate the new generations, leading Christians to be bearers of the gift of faith. This is an instruction that at first was given attention using methods and habits appropriate to bygone times and that today is giving rise to evasion, and to culpable, difficult, and frustrating improvisation, to cutesy banalization. These are the imitations of this work of mercy.

The art of formation is marvelous and is proper to the Church, which is mother and teacher. Its history is drenched with the works of the Doctors and Fathers and Mothers of the faith who are able to instruct and form, making flourish holy and true lives.

In the name of formation, instead, at times instruction leads to smartness, talking down to others, that invades in an unsustainable manner the attention of the other, inundating them with a knowledge they have not asked for and revealing only an unpleasant lack of depth.

To instruct the ignorant is mercy when, above all, we know how to do it.

Many there are who teach correct things without truly knowing them, and consequently are teaching them badly. They spit out stolen indications here and there, often cut from the saints, from popes or from wise persons, pawning them off on their neighbor without really knowing how to live them. These things smell false and trivialize true wisdom.

How many times have we seen important things debased because they have been on everybody's lips. Everybody teaches them, everybody says them, but there is no one who has actually lived them in the flesh.

Others teach correct things without considering the one who hears them, their language, with the effect of a topographic coincidence with the listeners, but not with the result of fruitful learning.

Should we open the sad chapter of the complaints of the people of God about clerical preaching? Pope Francis has magnificently addressed this theme in his programmatic exhortation, referencing it through an in-depth study of such a grave problem.[7]

When there is a lack of knowing how to instruct, the other can be offended by the instruction. They don't feel they're loved by the one who is training them, or at least, what the instructor is teaching doesn't save them, doesn't help them. The right thing could be said at

7    Pope Francis, *Evangelii gaudium*, November 24, 2013, nn. 135–39.

the wrong time or without adequate care for the outcome—that is to say, without verifying whether the other has been put in a position to understand.

These deficiencies open the path to inappropriate virtual teaching, through the media, which in reality are, however, only information, not formation, and where, obviously, informing doesn't automatically mean forming.

We should take note that it isn't easy to accomplish this work, and that the grave risk, from what we are seeing, is of causing harm. A person can be destroyed by distorted instruction.

It's necessary to underscore a fundamental aspect—namely, that we are dealing with a work that the Holy Spirit must accomplish in us, a wisdom that it's his to give us. And it's worth remarking that wisdom is a gift of the Holy Spirit, and in fact it's the very first gift, and it contains something of all the gifts of the Spirit.

And then a not-infrequent risk is to give off a wisdom that's merely human, not steeped in divine mercy. Through human expressions of wisdom, which are not at all without use and which are due the respect of which they're worthy, there are, however, the professionals. We pay them, and they take on their legal responsibilities.

At this point, we must talk about a work of mercy, not about any random type of teaching.

## INSTRUCTING AND PROVIDING FORMATION

Let's focus on two acts that the instructor needs to do and that are often not adequately distinguished: instructing and providing formation.

It's possible to learn without allowing ourselves to be properly formed, and it's possible to be formed without learning.

As an example, one day Peter shows that he has received instruction:

He said to them, "But who do you say that I am?" Simon Peter answered, "You are the Messiah, the Son of the living God." (Matt. 16:15–16)

Right after that, we read:

From that time on, Jesus began to show his disciples that he must go to Jerusalem and undergo great suffering at the hands of the elders and chief priests and scribes, and be killed, and on the third day be raised. And Peter took him aside and began to rebuke him, saying, "God forbid it, Lord! This must never happen to you." But he turned and said to Peter, "Get behind me, Satan! You are a stumbling block to me; for you are setting your mind not on divine things but on human things." (Matt. 16:21–23)

In the end, Jesus speaks to Peter and the other disciples:

Then Jesus told his disciples, "If any want to become my followers, let them deny themselves and take up their cross and follow me. For those who want to save their life will lose it, and those who lose their life for my sake will find it. (Matt. 16:24–25)

Peter has a fact, but not obedience to the fact. This is a reality made of knowing, but not of obeying, or having understood the instruction but not acting according to it.

On the other hand, there can also be an obeying but not knowing, being highly educated but ignorant. This is the case of the Pharisees, who have a meticulous, pragmatic observance of the law, but don't manage to recognize the Lord whom they are to obey. This is what in substance Jesus was to denounce in the terrible chapter twenty-three of the Gospel of Matthew.

Therefore, to instruct the ignorant is a refined work that implies information not only to saddle someone with, but rather to deliver wisely in order to cause the other to learn. It isn't a work that we invent; it's rooted in the Scriptures.

The heart of the Old Testament can in reality be recognized in the law, in Hebrew *Torah*, which has its origin in the verb *yrh*, which first of all implies "to see," but which can be traced back to the act of indicating a direction using the finger. By this it carries within itself the meanings of "indication," "prudence," "instruction," "warning," "way," or "path." Therefore, more than "rule," it refers rather to the reception of "wisdom."

Instruction is found at the center of the whole Old Testament. Psalm 119:97–99 says:

> Oh, how I love your law!
> It is my meditation all day long.
> Your commandment makes me wiser than my enemies,
> for it is always with me.
> I have more understanding than all my teachers,
> for your decrees are my meditation.

In turn, Jesus was a teacher—in fact, "the" Teacher.

In John 14:6, Jesus speaks in a strange way about knowing the way: *I am the way, the truth, and the life.* This text talks specifically about true knowing, but knowing what? What is Jesus's true teaching? He still speaks through another teacher: the Holy Spirit. Again it seems that humans have need of being disciples, those who learn.

The human condition, indeed, isn't to place ourselves in front of life as a teacher but as one who always has something to learn. As Matthew 23:8, 10 says:

> But you are not to be called rabbi, for you have one teacher, and you are all students. . . . Nor are you to be called instructors, for you have one instructor, the Messiah.

In the closing of the Gospel of Matthew (28:19–20), Jesus assigns three actions, of which two are linked to instruction:

> Go therefore and make disciples of all nations, baptizing them in the name of the Father and of the Son and of the Holy Spirit, and teaching them to obey everything that I have commanded you.

Teaching, instructing, baptizing, as I've said, show that two out of three imply assigning, *traditio*—Latin for "delivering"—wisdom. The Church is mother for baptism and teacher for the other two indications.

But how is it possible that seminarians are not instructed in how to instruct? What has happened in order for them not to be trained in the *munus docendi*—the gift of teaching?[8] At least there was a time when seminaries taught rhetoric, pompous but adequate for reception by the people. We think about Mussolini with a rhetoric that today, if we look at it again, looks like a comical film, but then it had an indisputable devastating efficiency.

Instead, today, training in the faith is left to the hormonal endowment of the candidates.

## ALWAYS OPEN TO THE NEW

What would it be to learn to be good instructors in the faith? At least the first and greatest difficulty that must be confronted is that the instructor must be instructed. . . .

To receive wisdom, to be trained, indeed represents a trauma: each of us already has, in fact, our own wisdom; there is no one who is truly simply ignorant. There can be an unconscious ignorance, being wrong

---

8    The gifts of ordination to the priesthood are three, called in Latin *tria munera*: (1) the gift of sanctifying—that is, of being the vessel of sacramental grace, in an eminently liturgical framework; (2) the gift of administering—that is, of governing in the communion the community or the reality that's entrusted to the priest alone; (3) the gift of instructing, of being instructors in the faith. *Munus sanctificandi, munus regendi, munus docendi.* Normally training is given in the first two, and historically, priests have never neglected them. But as for the third. . . .

without even knowing we are wrong, or to be ignorant because we are in a bad way, and we continue to blame the erroneous causes, not actually focusing on the fact that we're bringing out the bad within ourselves, or, worse still, that we're bringing it out in others, and thinking that's all right to do.

> When they came to the place that is called The Skull, they crucified Jesus there with the criminals, one on his right and one on his left. Then Jesus said, "Father, forgive them; for they do not know what they are doing." (Lk. 23:33–34)

The problem is that those who are ignorant don't think they're that way. In fact, it isn't a question of ignorance against wisdom, but of true wisdom against false wisdom.

On the road to Emmaus, Jesus had to work in a paradigmatic situation:

> Two of them were going to a village called Emmaus, about seven miles from Jerusalem, and talking with each other about all these things that had happened. While they were talking and discussing, Jesus himself came near and went with them, but their eyes were kept from recognizing him. (Lk. 24:13–16)

He isn't recognized, but he's noticed, not because he presents himself under another appearance, but because, as the text says, their eyes were incapable of recognizing him.

This dull gaze corresponds, we will see, to dull wisdom:

> And he said to them, "What are you discussing with each other while you walk along?" They stood still, looking sad. Then one of them, whose name was Cleopas, answered him, "Are you the only stranger in Jerusalem who does not know the things that have taken place there in these days?" He asked them, "What things?" (Lk. 24:17–19a)

It's impressive that Jesus is also ignorant—he doesn't know what has happened—or rather that he doesn't know it as they know it. He's the stranger who doesn't see what they see. And he asks them to inform him. He was himself instructed by ignorant persons. And some people say that faith isn't acquainted with irony. . . .

Here it's extraordinary that the two disciples delivered all the necessary facts, step by step, the very facts that later appeared as vivid proof of the opposite of what they were thinking at the time. But all the facts are under a distorted light: their expectation.

> They replied, "The things about Jesus of Nazareth, who was a prophet mighty in deed and word before God and all the people, and how our chief priests and leaders handed him over to be condemned to death and crucified him. But we had hoped that he was the one to redeem Israel. Yes, and besides all this, it is now the third day since these things took place. Moreover, some women of our group astounded us. They were at the tomb early this morning, and when they did not find his body there, they came back and told us that they had indeed seen a vision of angels who said that he was alive. Some of those who were with us went to the tomb and found it just as the women had said; but they did not see him." (Luke 24:19b–24)

It's here that everything becomes useless, under the perspective of their expectations, for them to answer, but they didn't understand that. And Jesus addresses an insult to the two disciples:

> Then he said to them, "Oh, how foolish you are, and how slow of heart to believe all that the prophets have declared! Was it not necessary that the Messiah should suffer these things and then enter into his glory?" (Lk. 24:25–27)

"Foolish" is a strong insult in Judaism; it means "bad," "crooked," "tortuous."

These disciples demonstrate that they possess their own interpretation of the facts; Jesus admonishes them so that they will change their reading of them. They have made a typical mistake: confuse the promises received with their own expectations.

This is the challenge that the ignorant must face: to change their own vision of the matters of fact, letting themselves in a certain sense be insulted, recognizing that they're foolish, slow to understand, opening themselves up to a surprising prospect and abandoning their own synthesis of the facts.

That's how it is. Every time I listen to the Word of God, each time I pray, each time I place myself in the presence of God, I know, I must remember, that I'll have to find myself to be foolish and a bit crooked. I don't enter into the liturgy to stay what I am, but to let myself be challenged and to allow myself to be instructed. I must also beg God to insult me a little, to challenge me, according to his parenthood, in order for me to take a small step outside of my deceptions, which are always still so many. If he so desires.

Fr. Amedeo Cencini speaks splendidly, with a happy neologism, of *docibilitas*, the capacity to learn, meaning the attitude that lets another be able to teach us something. Happiness is directly proportional to our capacity to be surprised, to learn things anew:

> Formation does not take place outside the world, but it is formation to be in the world, in this world, with its wounds and contradictions, with its questions and aspirations, with its unprecedented and unforeseeable newness.

There is an "always" and a "new" as God's dwelling.

> The young person must understand that very often it is actually sudden, radical changes that provoke faith and favor its daily development and prevent them from simple repetition without going on to take nutrition from the Word and from the events of the day. They must make themselves aware of the temptation to

shut themselves off from God's newness, to accustom themselves to a certain image of the divine, to use religion to avoid changing their minds and hearts and understand that the God of yesterday is the idol of today.[9]

If I don't open myself to the new, I learn nothing. This is simply evident.

The gift of a holy ignorance allows humans to reopen themselves constantly to what they don't know, and thereby to grow. Death, from this point of view, will be the last and the greatest surprise when it reveals heaven. Life is a school, a series of lessons to be received, and fundamentally it's the preparation for that moment, the last and definitive lesson, the most beautiful of discoveries: the Father's face.

But the urgency of opening ourselves to another wisdom is symmetrically linked to the action of the instructor, which is loving and desiring true good for the other. Instruct and love: but to do this we need in turn to have lived through the trauma of letting our own erroneous vision of the good be challenged, to be in turn recognized as being ignorant and in need of learning what the true good is.

Instructing is an act of love, as we have already seen. It implies two phases: having lived through the "trauma" of learning and therefore being familiar with its rigors and satisfactions, and then we will proceed with tenacity together with patience. We need always to remember how difficult it is to place ourselves under discussion.

The other phase is to instruct in what is needed, and this implies that one doesn't simply instruct, but that one instructs another. The other is the center of formation strategy. Content isn't enough; it's required for the content to be delivered to that quite specific hearer. It's required to have a feeling of feedback, to understand what is happening and to be acquainted with the true needs of the one who is listening.

They say that the difference between expert preachers and inexpert preachers is that the latter continue to speak until they have said

9   Amedeo Cencini, "La formazione in tempi di rinnovamento" [Formation in a Time of Change], February 25, 2007 article quoted on the website https://bit.ly/2up883e.

everything they know, while the former stop talking as soon as they have said what is needed. What a blow this is to verbose preachers like yours truly. . . .

## THE WISDOM THAT HUMANS LACK

There remains one point to confront: What is true ignorance? What is the wisdom that humans lack? Because, in the end, are we always learning?

At the end of his prologue, John writes this sentence (1:18): "No one has ever seen God. It is God the only Son, who is close to the Father's heart, who has made him known." There is something that we don't know enough about—namely, that only Christ, through the Holy Spirit, can reveal the Father.

He knows how to reveal him because he's in the Father's heart; he's the image of someone who is leaning their head on their dad's chest; he's the child rocked in the strong arms of the father; he's the image of the son or daughter. It's only he, the Son, who can reveal the Father.

Many people think of the Gospels as a collection of things to know, as information. Jesus, the teacher, teaches differently; he aims to teach, not notions, but the love of the Father.

In the same Gospel of John (5:19–20), Jesus says:

"Very truly, I tell you, the Son can do nothing on his own, but only what he sees the Father doing; for whatever the Father does, the Son does likewise. The Father loves the Son and shows him all that he himself is doing; and he will show him greater works than these, so that you will be astonished."

It's the grace of God that teaches the marvelousness of changing one's life. In the Letter to Titus, St. Paul wrote the proclamation that today is made on Christmas night:

For the grace of God has appeared, bringing salvation to all, training us to renounce impiety and worldly passions, and in the present age to live lives that are self-controlled, upright, and godly, while we wait for the blessed hope and the manifestation of the glory of our great God and Savior, Jesus Christ. (Tit. 2:11–13)

Grace is the love that changes human lives and direction; it's the capacity to understand the Father anew. It doesn't deal with intellectual deepening but rather with an existential change.

To instruct means to write and to sculpt in the heart of the other, in its innermost depths, the love of the Father. It's Christ who brings the truth of that love:

"You say that I am a king. For this I was born, and for this I came into the world, to testify to the truth. Everyone who belongs to the truth listens to my voice." (John 18:37)

The disciples are sent to carry out this work by training and instructing. Humans actually learn though deeds, through the wisdom of educators who cause them to have the experience of true learning. It's hard to see someone learning something only because it's explained to them. We learn when we've set our minds to doing something. The educator indicates things to do; the teacher gives an exercise in order to bring about change.

The true teacher, as Jesus shows, is the one who teaches God and his love by putting it into practice, not through a concept—for that a book is enough. The instructor isn't one who provides a simple lesson, but is one who through instruction loves the other, with the merciful treatment shown by a person who seeks to understand how to make the other person comprehend the reflection of God's love that's capable of shining in the hearts of all who need to discover it.

The principle of formation is that all persons are gifts from God; they're his work, his masterpiece. The art of the educator is that of furnishing elements that announce the uniqueness of the human person, who is God's handiwork.

A last question: What training is needed to arrive at carrying out this amazing handiwork? If the teacher par excellence is Christ, why in the world is he that? As we saw a short time ago, it's because he's the only one who can teach the most important thing: the Father. And why? Because he's the Son; he knows him; he can reveal him.

The best training is to know how to point out the Father and to be his children—to be intimately acquainted with him. Then, for sure, if you have truly known him, when you talk about him, tenderness will rain down from everything you say. And whoever listens to you will learn the most important thing: that the Father is marvelous.

# 3

# ADMONISH SINNERS

What disasters have been carried out in the name of this work! How many dark ghosts of unlicensed inquisitors, but also licensed ones, invade our imagination thinking about the authorization to correct our neighbor, to the perfectionistic and moralistic fury with which generations have grown up, censured from the outset, with the conviction that complaint and reprimand are still and always legitimate acts.

Ah! What have we done with Christianity, making it become the ethic frustrater of society: the commanding religious reprimand stems from self-castration!

How many instructors there are who, not knowing truly how to cultivate hearts, have resolved the educational dilemma through recourse to the sense of guilt, fired in all directions, indiscriminately.

With what fruit? Scarcely had the world emancipated itself that it kicked out this exercise of moralists, hating every censure in a manner that's just as furious. And the result isn't balanced, sadly, but equivalent in ugliness: no limit, nothing is bad, the very concept of sin is to be abolished, destroyed, torn up.

And people sink into the gorges of self-destruction without even being able to suspect that it's harmful, because there is nothing about which it can be said, "It's wrong." What? Who? How is this allowed? The intolerance of tolerance is as violent as moralistic inquisition.

To clarify what this work is, is rather momentous. But it could be that a bit of all of Christianity needs demystification, because it suddenly has a double fire of misinterpretation on the part of immature Christians, as Galatians 5:1 says: from freedom they have submitted again to a yoke of slavery with their guilt-producing, perfectionistic suffocations, full of common post-Enlightenment places steeped with generalizations that are often sentimental, fleshly, and infantile.

On the one hand the sense of admonition has been massacred, whereas, as we will see shortly, it should in reality be interwoven with care, with tenderness, with a healthy concern for the health and salvation of another. On the other hand, we have witnessed the pulverization of the sense of sin, or error, in its existential meaning: that of disaster, of tragedy.

Of admonition we retain the perverted sense of an aggressive interventionism. Of sin its secondary ethical and legal aspect has been overblown.

What butchery! Perhaps it's better to actually skip over this work? Do we have the necessary conditions to be able to talk about it?

We will try—somewhat, as with all the things that are in this volume—precisely to try, humbly, to give a bit of light; precisely, to demystify. In the end it's this that we are always trying to do, in this area.

## "CONVINCE OF SIN"

The verb *admonish* comes from the Latin *ad-monere*, to give a warning, an admonition. The image is that of a person whose life is at risk and someone saves that person by warning them.

The sinner, on the other hand, is one who has a "lack." "To sin," in fact, in the biblical concept, signifies "to miss the mark" of our own acts, to find oneself in a flawed dynamic that brings humans to an existential wandering away from our destination. This is why, in the loftiest form, sinners are also called "wanderers."

Do we need this work? Can we do without it?

It's useful to us to be familiar with a verb, *elenchein*, used both in the New Testament and in the Greek version of the Old, which means "convince of sin." This is a key verb for this work of mercy. Psalm 81:8, which uses it, gives a good expression of admonition: "Hear, O my people, while I admonish you; O Israel, if you would but listen to me!"[10] It's God who speaks to the people, hoping that they will open their hearts.

Psalm 81 continues (vv. 9–10):

There shall be no strange god among you;
    you shall not bow down to a foreign god.
I am the LORD your God,
    who brought you up out of the land of Egypt.
    Open your mouth wide and I will fill it.

The God of Israel spells out the devastating drama of idolatry, of placing trust in empty, lifeless things, and recalls that by contrast he has been a liberator, a father who provides, who desires to satisfy his people.

But God doesn't succeed in finding a hearing (v. 11): "But my people did not listen to my voice; Israel would not submit to me." And later he describes how good this would be for the people (vv. 13–16):

O that my people would listen to me,
    that Israel would walk in my ways!
Then I would quickly subdue their enemies,
    and turn my hand against their foes.
Those who hate the LORD would cringe before him,
    and their doom would last forever.
I would feed you with the finest of the wheat,
    and with honey from the rock I would satisfy you."

How many times have we said about someone, "How much better it would be for that one, if they listened! We can't say anything to that

---

10 Tradition bears, literally, the meaning of the verb *elenchein*, which is "to bear witness against, to show the guiltiness of someone, to convince someone of their error."

person, they never listen anymore"? And how many times has this been said about us? . . . "If they would only listen for a moment. . . ."

Which is more tragic: the error itself, or shutting ourselves off from help to get out of it?

We have skipped over one verse of this same psalm in which a threat is issued, the hardest one that can be heard (v. 12): "So I gave them over to their stubborn hearts, to follow their own counsels."

The focal point, the truly distressful thing, isn't to be wrong, but not to be aware of it, to destroy our own life and be convinced of being on the absolutely right path, and it's here that the worst situation arises: to be abandoned to ourselves. A prospect, this, that demonstrates a terrible aspect of the affair: that of having lost the care, the momentum for someone, and to leave them in their error, not to help them. Let them be slain and die, if this is what is willed.

You don't want to hear me? And here I am talking to you? Go cook in your own broth!

Perhaps we've experienced the true love of friends, that for which one day you wake up from your deceitfulness and you discover that some of them have not given up on you. They've continued to stand with you and haven't stopped telling you the truth, even though you reacted badly and didn't listen to them. But they stayed there, and while not endorsing you they have nonetheless not stopped taking care of you. And by contrast you discover that others left you to yourself the moment they perceived you were in deceitfulness; they had no other recourse than to aggressiveness, accusation, rejection. Judgment.

And in the end, you ask yourself who your friend is. And perhaps you find you're even worse than those who have condemned you.

In friendship we need perseverance, not a blackboard chalking up who is good and who is bad.

There is cause to weep over this work.

We ought greatly to fear not having anyone who acts as an objective reflection, no one who reveals to us that we are throwing something away or ruining something else, losing our own salvation. But perhaps still more, we ought to fear not knowing how to speak with one who needs our oversight, our loving opinion. We should be horrified at having lost our motherly love for one who is close to us—so much so as to be able to see that one destroy themselves and think: it serves them right!—and not to know how to remain alongside them and try to help them anyway.

I'm afraid of my rage toward my neighbor, but that's still a relationship. I'm even more afraid of my indifference. That's death.

## ADMONISH, NOT ACCUSE: THE GIFT OF INTELLECT

As we've seen, the first dynamic that's capable of defacing this work is to change admonition into accusation, an action that brings us to emphasize the errors of the wandering one, attacking and accusing vertically from on high. This is a behavior that tends to be aggressive and destructive; it implies the conviction of having understood the error and therefore is an impetuous attitude, violently judging in order to unmask the other and rub the other's face in their shortcoming.

This system is condemned in the Sermon on the Mount in Matthew 7:1–5, in which Jesus says:

"Do not judge, so that you may not be judged. For with the judgment you make you will be judged, and the measure you give will be the measure you get. Why do you see the speck in your neighbor's eye, but do not notice the log in your own eye? Or how can you say to your neighbor, 'Let me take the speck out of your eye,' while the log is in your own eye? You hypocrite, first take the log out of your own eye, and then you will see clearly to take the speck out of your neighbor's eye."

This text introduces the problem of accusing the other, of pedantic attention concerning errors, but this rigorism is in reality correlated to a blindness and a problem with oneself. Why is it so delicious to look at and point out the errors of others? For some it's a true and proper sport, an activity that generates a whole world connected with that attitude we call gossip, making it one's business to be involved with other people's business.

But taking pleasure in noticing the sins of others is instead about our own uncertainty and insufficiency. By watching what the other is doing, we are seeking comfort and compensation. Having something to laugh at about in someone is a form of living with our own incongruities. Not to see the log in our own eye while pointing out the speck in the other's eye is a behavior that's clearly immature and useless.

We often witness acts of brotherly correction packaged with projections that are truly our own, which are in reality merely accusations and condemnations, but which absolutely don't respect acting out of *ad monere*—out of giving a warning that would save the other from danger. Satan, *satàn* in Hebrew, in Scripture is the accuser, the adversary who opposes by acting through the use of an accusation fraught with a sense of latent guilt that's capable of locking the sinner into their present state. Certainly, the work of mercy has nothing to do with an attitude bereft of love that results in assault, violently highlighting the error.

Then there exists, as we have seen, the abandonment of the other, which is contempt. But there is an ulterior drift, which involves holding back: to keep quiet in the face of the other's mistake. This is a sin of omission, and it isn't a merciful act. Deceitfulness is deceitfulness, and it should be called out. The ostentatious tendency toward a watered-down do-goodism that makes the situation fill with vapor and doesn't define the mistake even shows up as a veiled sadism; in reality it turns into tormenting the other.

If Satan acts at first by accusing, now he's an affable flatterer, a temptation that tends to minimize the sin and/or cause one to fall into a victimhood that expels and projects away from itself the responsibility for the actual sinner, with the result that they remain once more in their state. The characteristic missive obviously also embraces the reality of speaking behind someone's back, not saying to their face what we are thinking while secretly taking note of the other person's error. This is hypocrisy.

A similar conduct takes refuge from denial because it runs the risk either of becoming aware of being wrong in judging or of having the other respond by bringing up the errors of the one who is doing the admonishing. As we can see, either in the dynamic of accusation or in the dynamic of omission, there exists a blatant duplicity and an incapacity for relationship.

The inability to carry out this work is proportional to the relational rarity of having someone nearby who knows how to truly confront and correct, if necessary, methodically edifying the other. It's truly rare to communicate what we have in our hearts, and in general we are all on the side of political correctness, of not doing any harm, "decaffeinated" relationships that don't go anywhere, possessing that aura of privacy that in the end has as its consequence a disconnect.

These shortcomings no doubt contaminate even the activity of parents. Many parents are afflicted with a grave formational deficit. Not knowing how to correct their own children, they fall into a dichotomy that makes them either absent themselves or be excessively harsh. These are two sides of the same coin: an absence of formation doomed by goodness, or a violence dictated by inability. The first is an indicator of a lack of commitment; the second is an indicator of a lack of maturity.

Then we reach the point of finding that the act of admonishing is characterized by an ability to communicate, a knowledge of the language to use and of the timetable of the other, but above all by the confirmation of a desire to correct without any selfish motives. For this reason, it's incumbent on us to ask ourselves a serious question: Do we desire to correct someone in order to be more comfortable? Or is it because we really love the other and we see that person's beauty and preciousness threatened?

A preventive discernment should authenticate the desire for correction, because the goal must be love, desiring true good for the other. Admonishing in order to mask our own rage, perfectionism, pretense, self-esteem: this never justifies admonishment and clearly must be avoided.

Who if not the Holy Spirit through his gifts is able to enlighten the will by defusing falsehoods and possible blunders?

The first gift of the Holy Spirit that functions in the work of mercy we are dealing with is the *intellect*, the capacity of *intus-legere*—Latin for "reading within"—and of *intus-ligare*—Latin for "linking internally." That is to say, to see in depth, to perceive the innermost connections.

This gift contrasts with an attitude of judgment and condemnation, and Jesus bears witness to it in the story of the woman caught in adultery:

> The scribes and the Pharisees brought a woman who had been caught in adultery; and making her stand before all of them, they said to him, "Teacher, this woman was caught in the very act of committing adultery. Now in the law Moses commanded us to stone such women. Now what do you say?" They said this to test him, so that they might have some charge to bring against him. Jesus bent down and wrote with his finger on the ground. When they kept on questioning him, he straightened up and said to them, "Let anyone among you who is without sin be the first to throw a stone at her." And once again he bent down and wrote on the ground. When they heard it, they went away, one by one, beginning with the elders; and Jesus was left alone with the woman standing before him. (John 8:3–9)

In the Talmudic ritual of stoning, the first one to throw a stone had to be the one who was accusing, the witness who assumed the responsibility of assigning blame. Jesus affirmed that only one who is without sin can be a sure witness, because sin makes us blind, incapable of seeing. Self-centeredness hinders us from being acquainted with the other, and it follows from this that to really understand the guilt of the other implies freedom from one's own ego, in order to see the other with the only gaze that is truth: the gaze of love. Only with this gaze, united with the *intellect*, can we become capable of receiving by intuition, not judging, in which the true problem is found, because often only the effects are corrected and not the causes of the behavior.

Love grants us the grace to understand people's hearts, making them feel accepted and listened to, even when we have recourse to speaking to them frankly. An attitude will show up that in Greek is *parresia*, the Christian art of communicating with freedom because we are prepared to lose everything for the other. In Acts 4:8–12 we see Peter has finally gained this *parresia* that makes him able, before the Sanhedrin, to unveil their error:

> Then Peter, filled with the Holy Spirit, said to them, "Rulers of the people and elders, if we are questioned today because of a good deed done to someone who was sick and are asked how this man has been healed, let it be known to all of you, and to all the people of Israel, that this man is standing before you in good health by the name of Jesus Christ of Nazareth, whom you crucified, whom God raised from the dead. This Jesus is
>
> > 'the stone that was rejected by you, the builders;
> > it has become the cornerstone.'
>
> There is salvation in no one else, for there is no other name under heaven given among mortals by which we must be saved."

Peter isn't afraid to express himself frankly, because he can at last bear testimony to the truth, no matter what it costs, and not fail to speak what he knows, because he has received the Spirit. And this *parresia* allows him to pronounce the truth not as a condemnation but as a hand stretched out to save, the act of offering a way out, the stone on which to rebuild after the error.

## FEAR OF GOD AND CORRECTION

The second gift of the Spirit involves the *fear of God*, that sense of risk that is a beautiful, healthy, warm, loving concern toward the other, who is unable to see that they're destroying themselves; this implies fear for the other, being afraid for them. The most essential aspect of this act is care for the other, troubling ourselves for them and using everything that there is and that can be had in order to be able to help them.

On the other hand, to be saved means—always—to accept being corrected, and this is something that doesn't put us at ease. We have inner snipers to protect our walls that possess great reactivity, and the bricks of our pride are quite thick. In Hebrews 12:11, St. Paul talked about the bitterness of correction: "Now, discipline always seems painful rather than pleasant at the time, but later it yields the peaceful fruit of righteousness to those who have been trained by it."

To welcome correction is very difficult. So many times, the one who corrects does it badly, but nonetheless if we take it in the right way, it can always be useful. It can make us grow, even when it's done badly. But it requires an attitude that's one of our old acquaintances, one that's fundamental in the one who corrects and in the one who is corrected: humility.

To expect from the outset that the other will welcome what is said to them is always a somewhat exaggerated claim. The correct attitude wants us to desire to bring the other to save themselves from their own errors because we are humbly conscious of needing to save ourselves from our own. The famous log in our own eye. Correcting someone arises primarily from correcting oneself. Before combatting externally, we first have to do battle inwardly.

There is a passage from the tremendous St. John Chrysostom, who, in the catechesis to those who are going to prepare for baptism, affirms:

> Reprove anger, placate furor. If someone has committed injustice, if someone has used violence, deplore it. Do not scorn it; pity it. Do not about go in fury and do not say, "I am undergoing an injustice in my soul." There is no one who undergoes injustice in the soul, unless we commit injustice to ourselves in the soul, and I will explain in what way.
>
> Is someone taking away your inheritance? That one has not committed injustice concerning the soul, but concerning riches. But if you on the other hand hold onto rancor, you have committed injustice toward yourself in your soul. Indeed riches taken away have not hurt you at all; they have stood you in good stead. Whereas you, not having put away your ire, will then give account for this rancor.
>
> Someone wronged you and mistreated you? That person has not committed injustice concerning the soul at all, but scarcely concerning the body. Did you reciprocate the mistreatment? You committed justice to yourself in the soul, having to give account for the words that you pronounced.
>
> This especially I would like you to know, that no one can commit injustice to yourself in your soul, not even the devil.[11]

Devastating. Note this well: *soul* in Greek is called *psyche*. . . . Do I really need to add a comment to this text, the tombstone of all victimhood?

---

11  John Chrysostom, *Catechesis on Baptism and on Mysteries*, first Catechesis, 31–32.

When we start from our need for correction, and we know well that, as St. John Chrysostom says, the true interior wound is something we do to ourselves, then we will know humbly how to approach the correction of our brother or sister.

## BROTHERLY CORRECTION

Here is our principal character, until now kept behind the curtain: brotherly correction. Let's address this act, which at times becomes a monster with seven heads, and somewhere else becomes an inert amoeba.

The chief text that concerns our work of mercy is Matthew 18, the chapter on communion between the church and our brother or sister. Here are verses 15–18:

> "If another member of the church sins against you, go and point out the fault when the two of you are alone. If the member listens to you, you have regained that one. But if you are not listened to, take one or two others along with you, so that every word may be confirmed by the evidence of two or three witnesses. If the member refuses to listen to them, tell it to the church; and if the offender refuses to listen even to the church, let such a one be to you as a Gentile and a tax collector. Truly I tell you, whatever you bind on earth will be bound in heaven, and whatever you loose on earth will be loosed in heaven."

Let's begin by observing the deformity of our church practice. What I've usually seen in the Christian community is something like this: if one of your brothers or sisters commits a fault, first you talk about it on the street, and everybody talks about it, and consequently someone who knows that person will find out about it. In the end someone will have the courage to speak to that person as well. . . .

The Gospel says, obviously, the exact opposite. And there is a very important expression, that we ought not to let ourselves run away from: when a brother or sister commits a fault, you seek that person out first: "If the member listens to you, you have regained that one." Regain. A strange expression.

Many people go to a lot of trouble to gain money. Other people change features to gain the esteem of others. Other people wear themselves out to gain position and security. Here there pops up a strange avarice: to regain one's fellow.

To seek out one's brother or sister. It's one thing to speak in order to dot the i's and cross the t's; it's another to speak in order to regain, recapture, the heart of a brother or sister. This is the art of not losing our own brothers and sisters.

If a brother or sister dies, you discover that all the things about which the two of you were not in agreement counted for absolutely nothing. You have lost a brother or a sister. Your heart breaks, and you'll never fix it again. The rest of your life a piece will be missing, and only in heaven will you find it again. And how many things lose their importance.

Yes, we need to think about heaven and about definitive things. In fact, the text didn't stop there. Let's reread the last part: "Truly I tell you, whatever you bind on earth will be bound in heaven, and whatever you loose on earth will be loosed in heaven."

Who knows why everyone thinks about power when this text is read? . . .

This is what we are talking about: on this earth I have ties, according to the status of true human relationships, which are insoluble ties, such as parenthood—because a child will never stop being your child—or such as the ties of siblings—because your sister will never be no longer your sister—because, let's repeat, true relationships are insoluble. But they can be betrayed, renounced, and then one is dissolving something on this earth. This is true even in heaven. Faithfulness and unfaithfulness to relationships are things that are in God's sight. On this you can stake heaven. I can erase from my life this brother or sister who has displeased me, but this deed doesn't disappear. It's there, and before God this will count; its record on the database will not be erased up there.

Baptism, Eucharist: these make us the body of Christ, even if we don't focus on it, and they make our lives something that makes "heaven" present: every Christian act is the salt of the earth that can give glory to God or can be worthy of being trodden under foot. Can people find faith through my Christian acts? Yes, thank God. But can people also lose faith through my non-Christian acts? Yes. Undoubtedly.

Am I seeking out my brother or sister when I speak? Or am I looking for justice?

Seeking is an act of a certain type. There are a pair of essential parables about "seeking." Let's look at one from Luke 15:8–10:

> "What woman having ten silver coins, if she loses one of them, does not light a lamp, sweep the house, and search carefully until she finds it? When she has found it, she calls together her friends and neighbors, saying, 'Rejoice with me, for I have found the coin that I had lost.' Just so, I tell you, there is joy in the presence of the angels of God over one sinner who repents."

The eagerness with which this woman seeks the lost coin, like the shepherd who seeks the lost sheep, speaks of an attitude: I seek until I find you; for me nine or ten are not the same. I know that I have ten; I am not making anything up; no one leaves here until we find the coin. Here we will not break off the search until this brother is found. I can't do without him.

If a mother or a father loses a child and doesn't find the child, they don't say, "It's all right, we have two others; two or three is more or less the same. . . ." Who would ever say that? Until they find that lost child, they lose a year of their lives for every ten minutes more that go by.

This is what it is to seek a brother or a sister. It's a matter of life and death.

Go talk with people who can't find someone. A young woman I know lost her husband after three months of marriage, over which I had presided. He left the house one day; they found his motorcycle.

Nothing. That happened several years ago. Put yourself in that situation, if you have any heart.

This is what it is to lose a brother or a sister. Think whether today we're going to find them. This is what it is to find a brother or a sister again.

If you came to know that somewhere I can find my brother who died twenty-five years ago, do you think that I would continue to write all this? Then again, I might be able to find so many other lost brothers. . . .

Relationships are lost through attitudes of mutual, hypocritical flattery. We don't talk about it; we don't truly meet each other. To regain a brother or sister implies the truth that isn't the act of going to admonish them so they understand what a stinker they are, but to regain them, bring them back, have them once again close to our hearts as brothers or sisters. And see them happy. That's the truth about seeking the lost one, not the pedantic preciseness of our explanations.

And surely, we will not fail to note the words of Matthew 18:17: "If the offender refuses to listen even to the church, let such a one be to you as a Gentile and a tax collector." What does that mean? Many people hold this text in a highly traditional interpretation that authorizes excommunication, expulsion from the Christian community.

It can't be denied that the practice of excommunication has a basis in Scripture, but this isn't that text. What? What is he saying?

I say: in St. Paul we have the basis for the practice we have just mentioned. We can certainly see this in the text of 1 Corinthians 5:1-5, for example, and its parallels, to take note of such an extreme remedy, which in any case is thought to be the last recourse for regaining a brother or a sister. But this text talks about something else.

We are in Matthew. Our text says that if the member refuses to listen even to the community, "let such a one be to you." Let's note the return of the singular, a personal, relational outlook, not one based on community, "as a Gentile and a tax collector." In Italian this is rendered

88

as "*the* Gentile and the tax collector." Not "a" Gentile, but "the" Gentile. What is the tax collector, what is the Gentile, for Matthew?

"You have heard that it was said, 'You shall love your neighbor and hate your enemy.' But I say to you, Love your enemies and pray for those who persecute you, so that you may be children of your Father in heaven; for he makes his sun rise on the evil and on the good, and sends rain on the righteous and on the unrighteous. For if you love those who love you, what reward do you have? Do not even the tax collectors do the same? And if you greet only your brothers and sisters, what more are you doing than others? Do not even the Gentiles do the same? Be perfect, therefore, as your heavenly Father is perfect." (Matt. 5:43–48)

The Gentile and the tax collector are those for whom we give our lives, the enemy who is to be loved because God loves them. With some people we need to try to talk to them; but if they don't listen, we are to love them as they are, take them on and love them as Christ did. With some people we can talk about Christ, but with others we need to be him. You take them as they are; you have tried, but they don't listen to you. Don't throw them out, the Gospel says. At that point, you love them as an enemy is loved, without expecting them to change. This isn't such an unlikely thing. It's done quite often. Who knows how many times it has been done for us?

To admonish a sinner is an act of love—deep, gentle and courageous, tender. At the same time, it's strong; it requires understanding and a sense of the preciousness of the person. It asks the Holy Spirit to help us distinguish the desire to deeply love the one who is falling into error from that of wanting simply to give ourselves freedom of conscience. How many errors are pointed out without love or, on the contrary, how many are not said, while we continue to utterly condemn them at a distance, without entering into a relationship?

To admonish requires great attention to the other, true care for the soul, the heart, the life, the outcome, the happiness of the one who is our neighbor. Normally, although not always, a criticism or an admonition done with love is perceived immediately and makes us happy. By that we now understand that the Holy Spirit is a spirit of correction and consolation, as we will see shortly again in the work *comfort the afflicted*, and it's opposed to that malicious spirit that's so harmful, the spirit of accusation and flattery.

We all need to be lovingly corrected by someone who cares for us, by a thoughtful person who knows how to give a calm, quiet word. As James 1:20 says, "for your anger does not produce God's righteousness."

A person doesn't change direction because they have been bitterly berated, but because they have been helped to find their own beauty, their own authentic importance. To have such attentiveness we need a sublime way to discern, to see, to understand our brother or our sister. This is a work of mercy. It is to see the other with the eyes of God.

Here is what Benedict XVI has said:

> We learn to look at each other not only with our eyes, but with the eyes of God, which is the gaze of Jesus Christ. A gaze that begins in the heart and does not stop at the surface, that goes beyond appearances and manages to capture the deepest aspirations of the other: waiting to be heard, waiting for caring attention, in a word: waiting for love.[12]

---

12  Pope Benedict XVI, *Angelus*, November 4, 2012, alt.

# 4

# COMFORT THE AFFLICTED

Somehow everyone must find a viewpoint about pain. Because we all have to reckon with pain.

A widespread attempt is to try to eliminate it. As if that were possible. No, the pain of human existence can't be taken away, because pain isn't an evil in itself, but rather a result of evil. The most common mistake, in fact, is to confuse pain with our problems. Physical pain and interior pain are like a gasoline leak that ignites to warn the driver. Pain is a sophisticated biological and spiritual mechanism for signaling a problem, for attracting our attention to something that's wrong, broken.

Let's try to take away pain. We will no longer have people who take care of their own illnesses in time. We will no longer have the possibility of signaling existential disasters. Pain is a symptom, not the evil itself. Without symptoms diagnoses will not be made. Pain is a gift for us to save ourselves. To be in a bad way serves as an impetus to take care of ourselves.

Now, our modern society, groggy with cascades of narcotic remedies, physical ones but above all psychological ones, is a society addicted to its ills, that doesn't take note of its pain, because it's buried under a tsunami of distractions.

When pain exceeds the strength of the distractions, of narcosis, then we could even arrive too late, when the gangrene in the heart can actually not allow amputation, because there aren't enough healthy parts.

God can do anything, and "he brings up from the great abyss" (Tobit 13:2), but he can't force his salvation on anyone. This is the

91

sophisticated diabolical mechanism that we have fallen for: not so much refusing salvation, but rather accustoming ourselves to ugliness and taking it for granted, and having nothing to ask for. An army of men and women on the track, dead from mediocrity and indifference. And instead they could be so noble, so precious. But the reality nowadays is out there beyond the sea of narcotics.

Nevertheless, this situation never has the last word. In any event it's pantomime and not reality, and reality comes sooner or later to the surface, and Providence never lets it play the three-card trick; it always fishes up the right card. And we wake up. Probably in pain, but finally real, alive, conscious and not asleep.

How many times does pain make people grow, and it lays bare trivia and nonsense? How many people have started on their way because of pain? Yes, let's say immediately what is the goal: comfort the afflicted and help them to overturn the mechanism—that is, to go through pain as the result of evil, to taking advantage of the pain as a point of departure, as a beginning and no longer as an end.

The other dominating strategy in the face of pain, even if it's less than the preceding one, is *rage*. Looking for someone or something to blame seems to be a solution. Having someone to lash out at is a natural, mechanical impulse. But it serves absolutely no purpose. Because in my experience, all hearts, even through the most disparate and unimaginable paths, wind up having it out with the guilty one who is closest at hand: themselves.

Armies of enraged people seek to survive their extremely real pain with the fictitious solution of punishing the guilty party. Pain for pain's sake, because misery loves company. Once the supposed wrongdoer has been punished, everything is exactly as it was before. The dead one stays dead, but it still remains that "what is crooked cannot be made straight, and what is lacking cannot be counted" (Eccl. 1:15).

## THE SENSE OF PAIN

We truly need for someone to know how to "comfort the afflicted," one who knows how to speak to the broken heart, and there is no shadow of doubt that this is one of the most difficult works of mercy, a test bench for the quality and the depth of the heart.

The misery that this act relieves is, specifically, the pain that can be defined as "affliction," from the Latin *ad-fligere*—that is, to strike, but used here in the passive: to be struck, blistered, wounded. It's a state that requires liniment, help, succor, and this work speaks, specifically, of that particular comfort that must arrive at the heart of the afflicted one, because, whether it's a matter of an interior ailment or a physical one, comfort always touches on the inner experience, the awareness of the reading of the ailment that the other is suffering from.

The meaning of suffering and pain is the great challenge, and human beings from the beginning have looked for explanations and motives for their own sorrows. As is pointed out by the work of mercy "instruct the ignorant," physical pain can be hard, but if there is an explanation, we can bear it and the heart is serene. If, on the contrary, the pain has no explanation, then it becomes intolerable. Affliction has need of a word that fills it, directs it, of an indication that orients its understanding.

Like the other works, "comfort the afflicted" has imitations, and in particular it suffers from various things that imitate it, things that seem to perform the office of comforting but don't achieve it. Three specific deviants are commonly observed, three camouflages of the act of mercy: feeling pity for it, numbing it, and projecting it.

Feeling pity for the afflicted one can, on the one hand, be something opportune if it means entering empathetically into the person's affliction, weeping with them, sharing their pain. But there is the danger of slipping from the good position of empathy into victimhood, associating ourselves with the pain by emphasizing it and thereby strengthening its hand.

There exists a practice that produces a series of acts that sensationalize the pain. Think, for example, of the ostentatious mourning that was once traditional, whereby the mourner's torment was exhibited in order to make their pain visible and give it greater weight. This act is dangerous, because if on the one hand the pain is clearly welcomed, neither denied nor underestimated, taken in its dimension without trivializing it, on the other hand the exaggerated emphasis runs the risk of taking the one who is suffering and nailing them more and more into the condition of being a victim, the object of something absurd and unacceptable.

Victimhood, once it has been triggered, is that logic for which the person, feeling sorry for themselves with the complicity of others, remains stuck in the well of their pain, in a black narcissism that hinders them from starting back on the road to getting better. It's obvious that victimhood doesn't comfort anyone, but rather it adds problems to the problem.

The second drift from what this act should be is of a narcotic type, according to a mentality that we have already seen so strongly in our time. But here we are in the specifics of the direct, personal act, when we attempt to help the afflicted one by distracting them. Even this impulse, in its healthy meaning, isn't in itself an evil: sometimes de-centering the attention can help us find clear-headedness again.

But it's one thing to relieve congestion by helping the other catch their breath, and another to engineer alienation, enveloping the one who is suffering by attention that doesn't allow them to think, so that in fact we are at the point of removing for the sake of removing, plain and simple. This intervention is an impetus toward superficiality, and it's dangerous because the problem is postponed and becomes aggravated. Running away from a circumstance accentuates the problems, which come back in strength to knock on the door of the one who suffers, heightened this time by the sense of ineptitude, of not having confronted them yet. This approach makes them become ever more burdensome, harsh, absurd.

The third degeneration of the act of comforting is to invite the afflicted one to look at who is worse off. This type of comfort equates to comparing existence to a symmetry, as if there existed a pain meter and the classification of rotten luck. But what kind of help can it give me to consider someone who suffers more than I? Unless you want to help me realize that I am dramatizing something that's common—and, if that's true, this needs to be done and it helps.

But if, on the other hand, you are launching me into boastfulness about the pain of another, you could absolutely cause me to sink into an even greater lack of meaning. From this I ought to infer that since there are others who are more miserable than I am, I need to calm down and focus on brightening up. But no one can be all right out of a sense of duty! No, there are others who are worse off, so you ought to be okay! But this is an incorrect equation, and it takes away our foundation; that's not how this works. I am in a bad way and that person over there is in a bad way, maybe worse, but I am in a bad way, and there are no communicating vessels about those things.

Comforting requires a great balance that therefore avoids either victimhood or alienation or comparison with the suffering of other people's situations.

These erroneous approaches are remnants in part of human immaturity and in part of a "yogurt-style" Christianity, a "vintage" spirituality in which comforting action conceivably becomes only a reprimand, because the only existential lockpick is the good old sense of guilt, as we have seen elsewhere.

## JOB AND HIS FRIENDS

In the Scriptures we find the case of Job, the man who was made an object of unheard-of suffering, who loses everything—health, possessions, children—and starts asking himself why he bears affliction. In a series of discourses, three friends attempt to comfort Job, each of them providing, one by one, three lines of interpretation of his pain, chasing after each other and repeating themselves. But for each proposition Job has a rather reactive reply: all of these "friendly" men appear to be corrupted by fundamental errors. Horrors more than errors.

The first explanation is that pain is a consequence of a fault, and we must accept suffering because we deserve it. Eliphaz, Job's first bumbling comforter, in a line taken up again by the others, says:

> "Think now, who that was innocent ever perished?
>   Or where were the upright cut off?
> As I have seen, those who plow iniquity
>   and sow trouble reap the same." (Job 4:7–8)

And later, he says explicitly:

> "For misery does not come from the earth,
>   nor does trouble sprout from the ground;
> but human beings are born to trouble
>   just as sparks fly upward."(Job 5:6–7)

There is no middle ground: humans beget their own pain.

It's the same old story that those who are good are well and those who are bad are bad off. Moreover, Job doesn't fall into that category, because the reader knows from the opening of the book that Job is a good man: "There was once a man in the land of Uz whose name was Job. That man was blameless and upright, one who feared God and turned away from evil" (Job 1:1). No misdeeds have been recorded as having been done by him, and he, justifiably, was to point this out:

> "Turn, I pray, let no wrong be done.
>   Turn now, my vindication is at stake.
> Is there any wrong on my tongue?
>   Cannot my taste discern calamity?" (Job 6:29–30)

The affirmation of Eliphaz is that no innocent person suffers. But the Bible begins with two brothers, Cain and Abel, and Abel, the innocent one, is the one who has a bad ending. And then, in the most important story, the Exodus, the people of Israel are condemned to pain and to oppression by the pharaoh, and not because they were guilty. And how had Israel arrived in Egypt? Because Joseph had been made to suffer at the hands of his brothers. Was Joseph perhaps guilty? But when and how? Joseph was the just man par excellence! These are macroscopic examples, but the biblical story gives the lie to that reading.

But this point doesn't rest here. It can certainly happen that the cause of our pain has been an error of ours, but digesting the pain because, after all, we are guilty isn't a comfort, and it reduces God to the status of an agent of the government's tax collection service.

And even if it were true, even if I deserved what is happening, what good would that do me? Now that, quite justifiably, I've told you that you brought it on yourself that you are now in a wheelchair because of the way you were driving that blasted motorcycle, pray tell, now what are you supposed to do with that? As if a person were not already torturing themselves enough already. . . . I ought to know how to say something quite different from that!

The second comfort out of the mouth of Job's friends is that pain and suffering are useful for correction. This isn't a platitude; it's all too true. Eliphaz is still speaking, and he says:

"How happy is the one whom God reproves;
    therefore do not despise the discipline of the Almighty.
For he wounds, but he binds up;
    he strikes, but his hands heal." (Job 5:17–18)

True, everyone needs correction. Pain makes us grow. True. But Job's case is unfortunate. We have seen that he's portrayed from the start of the book as a righteous man, especially because the purpose of the book is to make these visions relative—we are lazily harnessing the toil of the biblical author.

The second friend—Bildad is his name—will continue both the first and the second affirmations, and will go on to say:

"If you will seek God
    and make supplication to the Almighty,
if you are pure and upright,
    surely then he will rouse himself for you
    and restore to you your rightful place.
Though your beginning was small,
    your latter days will be very great." (Job 8:5–7)

Which is to say, if you are a good boy and you allow yourself to be corrected, you'll see that then you'll be rewarded, but you must deserve it. Let's repeat: the book patently disproves that this is Job's problem.

And from this we understand one thing: these are sketchy ways of speaking. Eliphaz and Bildad don't really look at Job, and this is what happens when our replies are perhaps correct but also theoretical. Existential algebra. I come visit you who are suffering, and I spit out a slogan learned in my previous experiences. I haven't looked at you; I haven't understood what is happening to you. I place into a little box all my teeny-weeny schemes, and I give them to you out of my head.

Of this type, what do I say to my brother or sister who has a tumor? And what do you want me to answer? I ought to be looking at your brother or sister and enter into a relationship with them, and at that point I would tell them what my heart has to say, not yours, and assuming that your brother or sister does actually want to talk with an unknown person like me. . . . And what should you say to them?! Do you have a heart? Do you love your brother or sister? And tell them what you want; if you really love them, you'll see that you'll help them and you won't hurt them.

Those who have "the right answer": God deliver us from them. The answer to whom? Now or six years ago? Here or in some faraway place?

But how is it possible that someone doesn't recognize that there exists only reality, that abstractions are just hot air.

God is correcting you. Thank you. Great. Whoa. And now what am I supposed to do? I have my feet firmly planted, and I'm suffering and I'm being corrected, I'm being corrected and I'm suffering. Good night. Go away.

But yes, this is true, only that a person understands this little by little, and generally in the first person singular, and, frequently, only later on.

The third "comfort" possesses the greater, perniciously religious bearing, that of resignation, abandoning oneself to God's inscrutable plan. The third friend is named Zofar, and he says: the only wise one is God, and since God knows everything, resign yourself, because in reality nothing can be done against God's decision:

"Can you find out the deep things of God?
  Can you find out the limit of the Almighty?
It is higher than heaven—what can you do?
  Deeper than Sheol—what can you know?
Its measure is longer than the earth,
  and broader than the sea.
If he passes through, and imprisons,
  and assembles for judgment, who can hinder him?" (Job 11:7–10)

There is an old Roman saying, "When it's your turn to suffer misfortune, don't take it wrong." You have to resign yourself to the incomprehensible, which only God knows. But is resignation a Christian attitude? Etymologically, the word *resign* comes from the Latin *resignare*, from *re-ad-signare*, meaning "to hand back the seals," to abandon an assignment that has been entrusted to us. Resignation means abandoning the challenge of human beings who need to live with awareness and consciousness. The answer that a person who is suffering is looking for is of another type, one that's much deeper.

The motivations of the three friends manifest inadequacy in the act of comforting. They're mistaken, trivial, superficial, and foreseeable methods, and unfortunately, they're paradigmatic of so many explanations of suffering vaunted as being Christian.

## TRUE COMFORT: TO GIVE COMPLETENESS

Then what is the true comfort, neither flawed, nor hypocritical, not sentimental, nor whiny, that's capable of furnishing instruments by means of which we will know how to live through a time of torment? What is "comforting the afflicted"?

In Hebrew for "comfort" the term *nacham* is used, meaning "take a break, stop, find rest," or even "give refuge" to those who seek a place of peace where suffering ends.

Greek uses a verb with a preposition, *parakaleo*, "to call close by." And the name of the Holy Spirit, the Paraclete, is the name of the defender, the advocate—in Latin *ad-vocatus*, "one you call to your aid"—and he's the counselor, the inner teacher.

Even more interesting for our work of mercy is the Latin etymology *cum-solari*, translated badly elsewhere as "to be with the only one," whereas the ancient *sòllus–sòlus* doesn't mean "alone, only, solitary," but rather it means "complete, entire." This term produced the Italian word *sollazzo*, which expresses being filled, fed, satisfied. In fact, there exists a Latin expression, *solari famen*, which means "to feed, to make sated." So, *to comfort* is presented curiously in one sense of giving completeness, because, in fact, pain is deprivation.

Let's note that Jesus, in his greatest tribulation, before dying expressed himself this way: "When Jesus had received the wine, he said, 'It is finished.' Then he bowed his head and gave up his spirit" (John 19:30). In a single word using the perfect participle of the Greek verb *teleo*, which means "to arrive at the end," "to reach the target," Jesus expresses a completion of life, reaching an objective. What does that mean?

True comfort is the completion of the process that starts out from a state of deprivation, when the missing part is found, when we receive the complete meaning of the road of suffering. The comforter, in the Latin meaning of the term, is one who gives back the piece that was taken away from the suffering, confronts the impairment that made it unlivable, torturing, because it was understood in an incomplete manner.

Job's friends stop at the causes, whereas true comforters seek the part that God desires to give. After the Lord had manifested his greatness, Job replied (42:5), "I had heard of you by the hearing of the ear, but now my eye sees you." This was one of the many things that Job needed to see. He had not yet grasped it, but now he could contemplate it. God disapproved of the empty behavior of the three friends: "The LORD said to Eliphaz the Temanite: 'My wrath is kindled against you and against your two friends; for you have not spoken of me what is right, as my servant Job has'" (Job 42:7).

One who carries out the act of comforting is able to place themselves alongside the suffering one, showing them what they're unable to see and allowing them to open their heart, their gaze, their spirit, to another perspective, an integral deepness that gives completeness. We are talking about hope. But not in a generic sense of wishing that things will get patched up. Let's look closely at the difference between expectation and hope. Hope isn't something I produce, because then it would be a theological virtue—which means a gift of God and not a natural virtue—as contrasted with expectation, which comes from biology/psychology. Instead, hope is based on a promise. It's a high quality in comforters: they ought to know the afflicted one so well that they know how to bring back into that person's heart the thing that God has promised them and help them to see the pain as part of God's faithfulness.

It could be asked: And what should this comforter ever need to know? Nothing, only an act of mercy according to the nature of God, that makes eternity present, that reveals the face of God in the pain. Just that. Nothing remarkable. . . . But what have we done about behaving as children of God?! But do we really think that illuminating the highest acts that exist would mean more or less to improvise? But we need to pray for a lifetime to arrive at the works of mercy, and especially the spiritual one that requires, without any doubt, being moved by the Holy Spirit! To know how to touch the heart of an afflicted person so as to rekindle their hope that has been crushed is the work in question. It isn't for specialists, but for all who have been baptized. Otherwise we fall back into the compensations that we have mentioned above.

There is a path in human life that's the fulfillment of the promises received, and pain is often a crossroads of the accomplishment of God's work. If Christians don't know these things, then who is supposed to know them?

Let's make a point for a moment more: I don't have a rational reply for pain. I, as a man, don't know why people suffer, and I don't really have an explanation for my own suffering. If I try to do that, I fall into the cause-effect mechanism, and I produce the various answers mentioned above. I am not acquainted with satisfactory answers to suffering outside of the mystery of Christ. I don't understand any other path to find the key to the tragic problem of human life outside of the Resurrection of Our Lord. What would we do otherwise? I don't know any human, philosophical, or scientific answers that are not mediocre. Go figure if I can write a book on the works of spiritual mercy in order to succeed at making these things make sense, but do me a favor! It takes the Holy Spirit to comfort human suffering. If we could comfort others on the basis of our ability, why was there a need for Christ to come and take on himself our suffering in order to untangle it? Even he, on the cross, came to the point of "why have you abandoned me?"—to the lack of meaning.

The comfort that someone brings me in my pain must be the irruption of God himself, his way of looking at things, his perspective with respect to what anyone can produce. Let's take the Beatitudes as shown in Matthew 5:3–10; they're an example of looking at things that sees the facts in a complete way, and not by chance are they called the "Magna Carta" of Christianity:

> "Blessed are the poor in spirit, for theirs is the kingdom of heaven.
> "Blessed are those who mourn, for they will be comforted.
> "Blessed are the meek, for they will inherit the earth.
> "Blessed are those who hunger and thirst for righteousness,
> for they will be filled.
> "Blessed are the merciful, for they will receive mercy.
> "Blessed are the pure in heart, for they will see God.
> "Blessed are the peacemakers, for they will be called children of God.
> "Blessed are those who are persecuted for righteousness' sake,
> for theirs is the kingdom of heaven."

These are all premises that anticipate the other piece of the story, a present that opens up to the future that nonetheless is present here and now: "for theirs is the kingdom of heaven." Suffering, then, isn't immovable; it isn't an end but the beginning of a process that provides release from the static nature of pain.

Psychological suffering that nails us down, blocks us, is called *anxiety*, a word that refers to the word *corner* (*angolo* in Italian), a place from where there is no exit. One who is anxious lives a pain that leads nowhere.[13] How is it possible to oppose this negative dynamic? The Holy Spirit that Jesus announces in John's Gospel is precisely the one who performs this comforting paraclesis: "But the Advocate, the Holy Spirit, whom the Father will send in my name, will teach you everything, and remind you of all that I have said to you" (John 14:26). The Holy Spirit, in our case, teaches the afflicted one what they don't know, which in suffering is something that's still missing, that's arriving and must be revealed by

13  We can, in order to understand this better, analyze the behavior of the prodigal son in the parable of Luke 15, in which we see a good example of a confining dynamic: he found himself in a blind alley because he had squandered all of his goods "in dissolute living," in Greek *asotōs*, from *a* (a privative) and *sotōs*, which derives from *sōteria, salvation, solution*; the dissolute one is one who has no solution. Typical of evil is indeed placing ourselves in "dire straits," confining ourselves to an elliptical system in which a destructive "loop" repeats itself without any exit. The dissolute one squanders everything in search of a pleasure that never comes because he's caught in a self-destructive, agonizing dynamic.

announcing something in the future: "When the Spirit of truth comes, he will guide you into all the truth; for he will not speak on his own, but will speak whatever he hears, and he will declare to you the things that are to come" (John 16:13).

St. Paul was to develop this experience with these words:

I consider that the sufferings of this present time are not worth comparing with the glory about to be revealed to us. (Rom. 8:18)

For this slight momentary affliction is preparing us for an eternal weight of glory beyond all measure. (2 Cor. 4:17)

In the Hebrew language *glory* corresponds to the specific weight of things. To acquire depth. To have a depth that knows about eternity. If you see a person who has substance, depth, nobleness, you can wager that suffering has made that person so beautiful. There is something that I've said a million times to young people: If you can solve a problem, solve it. But if you can't solve it, it will solve you." If there is a smidgen of greatness in people, it generally comes from that.

But not automatically. Suffering deepens you if you embrace it. If you refuse it, it butchers you, that's all, and for nothing. For that reason this work is important, because it's a fork in the road at which either you can go toward the sublime, or you can degenerate.

The Holy Spirit, interpreting the meaning the Cross of Christ, reveals to humanity the missing part of suffering, the one that God transforms into profoundness, into newness, into development, into growth. Pain is certainly not to be sought out, but when it manifests itself we need to know how to embrace it as the start of a change, at times the abandonment of immaturity, but in any case, a precious instrument that God uses to construct something more serious, more true. In the ultimate analysis, heaven.

The cross is the gateway to resurrection. The cross and death were the prerequisites, but the Resurrection is the true result. As John Paul II, in the apostolic letter *Salvifici Doloris* (19), wrote:

One can say that with the Passion of Christ all human suffering has found itself in a new situation. And it is as though Job has foreseen this when he said: "I know that my Redeemer lives . . .", and as though he had directed towards it his own suffering, which without the Redemption could not have revealed to him the fullness of its meaning.

A process counts toward its goal, toward its point of arrival. When we suffer it's important for someone to help us to have in our heart the certainty not of an end but of a beginning. While pain and grief usually imprint a terminal thought, the Holy Spirit reveals in the Cross a departure, a start toward God's extraordinary plan.

Jesus was to transform what seemed to be an end, the tomb, into a point of departure. From this it follows that comfort is to discover that every human story is in God's hands, and he it is who leads it, carries it out, conscious that the mystery of the Cross doesn't stop existence, but it opens up our vision to the wonder of the Resurrection.

In pain, people seem like impatient flies who are looking how to get out of the jar, but it's necessary for suffering to take its course, and to let it complete its mission. Offering comfort is an exhortation to turn over the affliction to God so that it's understood that this is only one part of the story: the Cross is a way station; it's a "transitional location," wrote don Tonino Bello.[14] We always go further.

## COMFORTED IN ORDER TO COMFORT

Knowing how to comfort an afflicted person requires the personal memory of that Resurrection act, having stored up the good that has been received from our own sufferings. The persons who are truly able to comfort are those who have been comforted, those who have gained from their suffering a path of growth in faith, in hope, in charity—something noble, great, and beautiful. To place oneself at the side of an

---

14 Tonino Bello, *Il parcheggio del Calvario* (The Parking Lot of Calvary), in *Omelie e scritti quaresimali*, vol. 2 (Molfetta [BA]: Luce e Vita, 2005), p. 307.

afflicted person, improvising an interpretation, makes no sense; it's to indicate a path to take without ever having walked that path ourselves. That sounds false a mile away.

St. Paul eloquently explains the art of giving true comfort:

Blessed be the God and Father of our Lord Jesus Christ, the Father of mercies and the God of all consolation, who consoles us in all our affliction, so that we may be able to console those who are in any affliction with the consolation with which we ourselves are consoled by God. For just as the sufferings of Christ are abundant for us, so also our consolation is abundant through Christ. If we are being afflicted, it is for your consolation and salvation; if we are being consoled, it is for your consolation, which you experience when you patiently endure the same sufferings that we are also suffering. Our hope for you is unshaken; for we know that as you share in our sufferings, so also you share in our consolation. (2 Cor. 1:3–7)

The act of comforting derives from the experience of redemption of our own suffering. It isn't at all easy to give answers to the suffering of others. Prudence and patience are necessary. We don't receive comfort automatically but under the "escort" of having been left by life to work, having incorporated our own story. If we have not accepted something, if we are still shocked or outraged by some part of our life, what would we ever want to say? Words without any foundation. So it happens that many don't let themselves be taught by Providence but at the same time claim to know how to speak to others. I've often seen comforters who are more immature than those they desire to comfort. And when you are sick, by direct experience it's clear whether the one who is speaking to you has substance or not.

Let's look at the training of a comforter in a marvelous text from the prophet Isaiah (50:4–10).

The LORD GOD has given me
    the tongue of a teacher,

that I may know how to sustain
the weary with a word.
Morning by morning he wakens—
wakens my ear
to listen as those who are taught.
The LORD GOD has opened my ear,
and I was not rebellious,
I did not turn backward.
I gave my back to those who struck me,
and my cheeks to those who pulled out the beard;
I did not hide my face
from insult and spitting.

The LORD GOD helps me;
therefore I have not been disgraced;
therefore I have set my face like flint,
and I know that I shall not be put to shame;
he who vindicates me is near.
Who will contend with me?
Let us stand up together.
Who are my adversaries?
Let them confront me.
It is the LORD GOD who helps me;
who will declare me guilty?
All of them will wear out like a garment;
the moth will eat them up.

Who among you fears the LORD
and obeys the voice of his servant,
who walks in darkness
and has no light,
yet trusts in the name of the LORD
and relies upon his God?

One who possesses the tongue of a disciple who knows how to comfort a disheartened person is one who has learned to hope, to surrender himself to God while they're plucking out his beard, who has known closeness to God in solitude and in persecution, who can speak to one who walks in darkness, because he has also come from there.

As we have said, a spiritual work of mercy isn't an act of the will: I want to comfort you. Sure, thanks. But you do it if you have let yourself be carried by the Holy Spirit in the day of darkness. Otherwise, what are you talking about, dear brother, dear sister?

The theological virtue of *Hope*, the Church affirms, "responds to the aspiration to happiness, which God has placed in the heart of every person."[15] With intensity the recent pontiffs have exhorted the faithful to cultivate this virtue. One thinks of the famous invitation, "Be not afraid," with which St. John Paul II began his pontificate,[16] or of the marvelous encyclical *Spe Salvi* of Benedict XVI, of the "Do not let your hope be stolen" of Pope Francis,[17] just to cite a few examples. *Hope* isn't a positive, optimistic attitude. It isn't a feeling, but an act and a gift of God. In the depths of the human soul there lives a Light that in the midst of deep despair, in the depths of the heart, makes us conscious of a truth: life is precious, and we are not born for no reason. "And hope does not disappoint us, because God's love has been poured into our hearts through the Holy Spirit that has been given to us" (Rom. 5:5).

> Suffering as it were contains a special *call to the virtue* which man must exercise on his own part. And this is the virtue of perseverance in bearing whatever disturbs and causes harm. In doing this, the individual unleashes hope, which maintains in him the conviction that suffering will not get the better of him, that it will not deprive him of his dignity as a human being, a dignity linked to awareness of the meaning of life. And indeed

---

15  *Catechism of the Catholic Church*, 1818.
16  Pope John Paul II, *Discourse at the Beginning of His Pontificate*, October 22, 1978.
17  Pope Francis, *Homily*, 28th World Youth Day, Palm Sunday, March 24, 2013.

this meaning makes itself known together with *the working of God's love,* which is the supreme gift of the Holy Spirit. The more he shares in this love, man rediscovers himself more and more fully in suffering: he rediscovers the "soul" which he thought he had "lost" because of suffering.[18]

18  John Paul II, apostolic letter *Salvifici Doloris,* February 11, 1984, 23.

# 5

# FORGIVE OFFENSES

With "comfort the afflicted" we have finished the four works that allow us to practice mercy toward the heart of another. The next two, "forgive offenses" and "bear with those who wrong us," are mercy in bulk, free of cost. They don't imply that the other person understands or matures or learns or welcomes us. They stay the stinker that they are, the burdensome person who knows how to be so.

We can be suspicious, in the first four works, that by extricating a doubtful person from their doubts, or by causing the ignorant person to learn, or by straightening out a sinner, a person might be doing these things for themselves. Having someone else experience some kind of suffering that's getting better is something that can take a weight off our backs. It isn't that it's this for sure, but we can suspect that this temptation exists. But with the next two works we can't be misled; on the contrary, in performing them we don't gain any advantage.

Even so, we could turn the talk around: if we were to practice the first four without involving the next two, it's all a bit false. We think about a person who corrects someone who is in error or instructs an ignorant person but isn't willing to forgive that person or put up with them . . . that would be ridiculous hypocrisy.

We are pointing this out because when we approach another person to correct them or something of the kind, we have to declare in some way that we are doing this out of love. And this can be true or false. Only forgiveness will authenticate or not our declaration of brotherly love or some such. . . .

And so we open the chapter with false forgiveness.

Perfunctory forgiveness, bragging forgiveness, indefinite forgiveness, selective forgiveness, sentimental forgiveness, forgiveness from a position of strength, obligatory forgiveness, forgiveness for which we nastily take credit, churchy forgiveness, seeming forgiveness from the head but not from the heart . . . need we continue? It's an infinite list.

Forgiveness is a little like the one and only Sacher-Torte chocolate cake from Vienna that has been much copied in Italy, or like Guizza Cola, which is an imitation of the real thing: inflated and trivialized.

We always find ourselves in the usual misconception that pursues us from the start of our present adventure: to squeeze out of our nature that which is only received as a gift from God. And then our wretched assaults on forgiveness begin; these lead to two principal swamps: hypocrisy and superficiality. In the first one we find quite a case of church etiquette that includes communion using refined exercises of the facial muscles, a smile that borders on being grinding, because it's bad to declare oneself to be on a collision path. But separately its quorum of muriatic acid is regained, through the swing of the pendulum.

With regard to hypocrisy, many public declarations of forgiveness flourish. Often, they're ridiculous and easily identifiable as such.

But in my opinion the box of superficiality has more contents. Because ultimately most people want to undertake the practice of forgiveness, and then they scan their own wingspan and produce what they can, forgiveness concerning this but not that, or forgiveness that lasts for the space of a hormone surge, or mercy like acid reflux— sweaty, fraught with eruptions from their innards, said to be hernias.

In Naples they say, "*Ma se po' campà accusì?*"—meaning, "But can you really live like that?"

Many people attempt to do it. Badly.

## THE NEED FOR FORGIVENESS

Where is this cynical reflection taking us? To the need for forgiveness. Which is to say: the problem of absolving the wrong in another isn't a luxury. It isn't a product of an existential upper class. No. Without forgiveness for wrongs received, we are stuck. If we are walking, we stop on the spot. We get nowhere. Everything we don't forgive beats inside us like a person buried alive. You could even write a book on the spiritual works of mercy, but either you have forgiven the wrongs done to you or you have not. And imitations don't work.

And in many ways, we are still in midstream: we still have to arrive at the place of accomplishing our mission. But we can be more or less on the way.

But look at what a contradiction this is: without forgiveness we can't actually unlock the very tissue of human beings, and at the same time we don't have forgiveness as our basic structure; it's something that we receive and not something we produce ourselves.

Let me be clear about something.

*"He forgives all your offences"* (Ps. 103:3 njb). The words of this psalm magnificently express the greatness of this work of mercy because, in reality, forgiveness is actually the act that's closest to the heart of God, a grace given to us from his merciful love that allows our relationship with him, and consequently with our neighbor, to live. These are two aspects that represent the center and the very aim of human life.

Therefore, to understand what "forgiving offenses" is and what it involves, we need to repeat the axiom mentioned above: forgiveness isn't optional. No human relationship is possible without forgiveness. No relational truth and authentic frontality is thinkable without bearing in mind the propensity toward doing wrong that affects the human heart and for that reason makes the antidote of forgiveness even more necessary. Where there is present a somewhat feeble consciousness of that necessity, one way or another the need to be forgiven seems more urgent than the need to forgive. We will see that this is true genealogically, but not existentially.

As always, we ought to pay attention to the human pattern of altering the truth of the act of mercy, quashing grace and rendering ineffectual the action of true forgiveness. This condition calls for diagnosing some falsifications that lead to the implementation and the scope of the merciful action itself.

Within the framework of an offense—for example, within a relationship—we very often witness what can be defined as "forced removal"; *to remove* means to keep the offense received far away from our own conscience, disregarding it and keeping our distance from it. But this is a risky process for the human soul because it doesn't consider the fact that the injury remains present nonetheless, and for this reason we don't understand when and how it will present itself and in what form.

The second alteration aims instead at negating the offense, maintaining the relationship in a limbo that's even more opportunistic, causing the death of the relationship itself. But the wrong that's done or sustained is such that it can be neither denied nor sugarcoated with a vain do-goodism that sooner or later will lead to rage.

In a similar manner we lapse into rational activity that seeks to understand the other. But this also reveals itself to be lacking, even counterproductive, because to put ourselves into another person's shoes can actually feed still more our inclination to feel as if the other person owes us something as a result of our being able to make that observation. We can think that after due consideration, we would never have done an offensive action like the one we have received.

These deformations reaffirm something substantial—namely, that the work of forgiving offenses isn't about human goodwill. The error is actually that of drawing upon ourselves. As a rule, we always start from the will, which seeks to feed on feelings of compassion toward those who have done wrong, but these impulses are subject to change. They don't continue; they're fragile and unstable.

We can try to peer a bit into the human, horizontal mechanism of forgiveness. I remember a case brought to me by a friend of mine, an excellent psychotherapist and psychiatrist, who justly defended his art, which is more than legitimate. I have nothing against psychoanalysis; it's a good and necessary thing, but it has its area of relevancy: balance, not happiness. Balance is vital, but happiness belongs to another type of reality.

This friend of mine and I were talking about the happy outcome that therapy produced in a man who had been the object of violence by his father. When he started therapy, he had been destroyed and was full of bitterness, incapable of holding anything outside of the contamination of his hatred of his father. That man, through a therapeutic journey of consciousness and growth, had transformed into positivity all the wrong he had undergone: by founding a nonprofit organization for the defense of the rights of mistreated children! Which is to say that he had not really solved the problem; he had sublimated it, on another level that was constructive, supportive, but still present. The driving force behind it was the same. This was not a resurrection; it was a reorganization of assets. As a rule, these are the best results. They are not to be sneezed at, because they go to a nobler level—but the wound is still there.

## THE FIRE OF WRATH

We need to keep in mind that the fire that fuels human difficulty in forgiving is called *wrath*, which consists in an unbalanced inner level, the sense of disequilibrium that we stigmatize trivially as "the desire for revenge."[19] We associate this with the conviction that we have been victims of something and that we need to restore justice by receiving redress for the wrong that has been done. These conditions drag with them the risk of slipping from victim into victimizer. The desire for justice turns us into executioners, and our bleeding wounds in some way open the door to sadism. From these excesses we see the subsequent risk that unresolved wrath is able to disguise itself as

19 *Catechism of the Catholic Church*, 2302.

rational justification for losing our sense of limits. An inward and outward disaster. Wrathful people live like that, and as a result there are so many of them walking around.

We repeat: the problem is that forgiving implies healing. As Sirach 28:3 says, "Does anyone harbor anger against another, and expect healing from the Lord?"

Let's set forth these three phases better.

The first is when the wrong comes over us and makes us feel like victims. This identification results in a black hole that it's extremely complicated to come out of. The torture of the wrong done to us crystalizes the person into a harmful state of moping around. This is deception that makes us live childishly, like whiny kids. So, what happens is we don't succeed in building a family, for example, or we interrupt relationships rather than, on the contrary, carrying them forward, through allegiances to the role of victimhood.

The wounds don't lie dormant, and often they're magnified, even if they appear to be the same. A priest friend of mine used to say that a blister in the mouth, when touched with the tongue, seems like a watermelon. But then when you look at it in the mirror, it's a speck. It's just like that: a speck turns into a watermelon. This is like falling in love with our own suffering, with a heart engraved on the trunk of a tree with our initial on one side and on the other the *S* of suffering. "You don't know how much I've suffered. . . ." And, frankly, I don't know what is so urgent for you to know it. . . .

How many people there are who swap love for medical assistance. And how many "nurses" and how many "Red Cross workers" run to help, exchanging love (which in itself would bring about the taking of responsibility for our troubles and for the offenses of others) for a welfarism that in reality feeds their own ego, making them the hero or heroine who by their acts saves the other person from danger and suffering.

The second phase is the desire for justice by which we begin to have a mind that becomes a balance scale: people who are perennially enraged, people who vomit recriminations, such as "Give us this day our daily enemy," someone to speak badly about, someone whose nastiness we want to emphasize. It's no surprise that the page that attracts the most readers of newspapers is the crime page. The facts about blood clamor to be identified and projected.

Justice becomes an emblem, but because of this people ruin their lives because comparison, which is the fruit of envy, begins to measure everything and every relationship: "My sister shouldn't have been cuter than me! She has a cute nose. . . . I have this nose. . . . Why is my brother handsomer and tougher? It isn't fair. . . ." Behind all this there is something that has not been forgiven.

The third phase is hoping for punishment. This is the sadism that comes after victimhood and vigilantism: "It serves them right!" We become the authorized hatchet men of others, ready to let the guillotine fall in pursuit of setting right the wrong or the offense.

There is something that needs explanation: How in the world are many people fascinated by films that show people who have been massacred, tortured, and the entertainment is their suffering? Just think about the fact that the monument that's the symbol of Rome is the Colosseum. What was it used for? A theater where the entertainment was sadism, meaning death. Why did people find pleasure in that? The compulsion of torture, so frequent in history, unjustifiable in a rational and serene mind—what seedy place does it trace back to in the human soul? How could people ever, in fits of rage, arrive at unimaginable violence?

I will never forget the day when I had to comfort a woman who had just witnessed the murder of a man because of a problem with parking, two steps from my parish in those days.

A humanity that has no familiarity with the process of reconciliation and has no familiarity with the way to disactivate sadism can prepare for a daily occurrence of micro-violence. If a man absolutizes his compulsions, it's possible for him to feel he's authorized to kill the wife he's losing control over.

Narcissistic-obsessive personality disorder is at the bottom of a horrific number of murders of women. Obviously, that's an extremely serious pathology, but if forgiveness is a great unknown, the floodgates are wide open.

In other words, by painting a black picture I am trying to emphasize that this sublime work is an absolute priority in our interior balance. One who doesn't forgive doesn't find peace.

## ONLY GOD CAN FORGIVE

What is to be done? How is this work carried out? What is this work, really?

True forgiveness can't spring up, let's repeat, from a simply voluntary attitude. That's because such an attitude doesn't hold sway over the inner strengths of passion and sin. Forgiveness is rooted in the depths of God's being: only God can forgive. Let's remember the Pharisee's question to Jesus in Mark 2:7: "Who can forgive sins but God alone?" We have seen that Jesus doesn't answer the question, but rather proclaims that he, Son of the Father, is bringing God's nature, the forgiveness of sins, upon earth.

Forgiveness is the hyper-gift—that is, the double gift. *Offense* is a word that comes from the intensifier *ob* and from the root *fen*, which is also connected to the term *funest*—meaning "causing evil or death." It indicates that which kills, that which wounds to the death. Forgiving, then, is to make a double gift to one who is deadly, to one who is funest, to one who offends, to one who wounds. It's the very power of Christ to take the offense, the Cross and the suffering that we give him, and restore it transformed into forgiveness, turning it into redemption. This manifests his breaking into the world: this is Easter; this is redemption.

Let's take care to focus better on the process that so many Christian men and women have experienced: the wrong that has been done to me I can't take away, but it's so much more funest to the extent that in reality it continues to mark my existence, because I can't forgive it. One who forgives escapes that consequence and is finally free from the wrong they suffered. They have made a qualitative leap, and this is a vital process of growth, quite connected to an encounter with the Creator, the One who knows how to forge a new heart, who knows how to give newness, for whom we are no longer stuck in the suffering of the wrong we have received.

We need to heal from all the wrong that we have suffered, just as we need to heal from all the wrong that we have done. Let's take careful note: this occurrence isn't an attitude; it's a path, a wide-ranging process. It means growing; it means going forward; it means retaking possession of our own heart. It means forgiveness toward those who have done wrong, and it means getting back in the saddle of our own lives and going back into action, not remaining passive in front of our own existence.

But the journey is secondly to return to the horizontal relationship, having first passed through the vertical relationship. Because, precisely, forgiveness isn't an independent, original act, not part of us. We are but poor creatures; otherwise, we claim to be capable of producing so much life that we can create reality anew. But that, obviously, God alone can do.

But what does it mean to start out with God? It means to start from the overriding necessity of being forgiven.

At first this will be incomprehensible for someone, but when I find myself facing a person who finds themselves unable to forgive, of course I welcome them and try to understand their pain and all that their heart full of resentment holds, but I also know that I am facing someone who doesn't have a fully adult relationship with God.

I must explain. People who are very mature in the life of grace, saints and so many other true Christians, who in general call little attention to their existence, have an acute sense of their indebtedness to God. Let's analyze more closely the word *debt*: from the Latin *debere*, it indicates being obligated to someone. It's worth noting that the New Testament introduces this category to describe the reality of sin, which in the Old was perhaps implicit, but not explicit. This makes us pass from a legal concept of sin—the transgression of a norm—to a relational concept—you have not respected our relationship and you owe me something: we have a problem between us.

We think this implies the weight of the gravity of sins. But this is still the legal concept. St. Thérèse of Lisieux did not commit a mortal sin in her brief life, but she had a highly acute sense of her need for God and of her debt to him.

If we ask a Sunday Christian about their pride, we could find the other has taken offense, replying in a way that shows they don't accept being examined. Soon they might say the classic line, "You don't know who I am," or something similar. If we asked St. Philip Neri about his pride, probably we would see him begin to grieve and to acknowledge his own arrogance. . . . The sense of our own fragility increases the more we measure ourselves against something sublime. If we measure ourselves against small-time obstacles, we are perfect. If we measure ourselves against God's love, we will always fall short.

A dear friend of mine, Carlo Striano, who now has gone to be with the Father, and from whom I learned to think about the things of God as a son and not as a slave, used to say that at the beginning of the spiritual life you weigh your sins in tons, but when you are more intimate with the Father, you weigh them in ounces and they weigh on you as tons. A coarse, unpolished soul will not notice many things; a mature soul will suffer from many insufficiencies in their love for their brothers and sisters and in their relationship with God. They will feel that there is still so much missing. In his *Commentary on the Song of Songs*, Origen said that relationship with God is like having "received the sweet wound of his arrow." If someone has tasted God's patience, they can't ignore it, and they never feel they're on top.

And this isn't an overwhelming, oppressive sensation, but rather it's astonishment, the joy of children, surprise, happiness at something much bigger than us.

In light of a widespread patristic and spiritual consciousness, it's worth asking ourselves questions that establish a framework for our state of indebtedness: Have we truly given all that we ought to have given? Have we been the children of God that we ought to have been? Have we been the Christians that we ought to have been? That part of the body of the Church that we ought to have been? Are we not truly indebted to the people who are around us? Have we been the people that we could have been?

I am not the priest that I should be, and I know very well that I lack so much to be the priest that I could and ought to be. In many things I owe a debt to the people I should be serving: of a greater love, of a much deeper attention, of a much truer charity. I haven't been the son that I ought to have been, and not the brother that I should be. People expect more love from me, and not an absurd pretense.

If we see ourselves in light of the people we have around us, are we not truly indebted to the sisters and brothers who show greater charity, who display a totally different sweetness, a deeper acceptance? When we let these thoughts enter into our hearts, in the end we become debtors and we stand before the Father, saying, "I haven't loved as much as I should love; I haven't given as much as I should give; very often out of fear or anxiety I held onto my life." At that moment we start out with God.

To look at ourselves this way entails suffering—there is no need to deny it. To set fire to the flaws in my behavior, to discover how much I am lacking because I measure myself against love and not against justice, can make me see the yawning gap of my fragility and the insufficiency of what I try to do. And this can lead me to a fork in the road: either to proudly disallow my weakness or to surrender it to the mercy of God. Spending life looking to show that we are on top of our challenges is called Pharisaism, in which anxiety shifts away from seriously having loved to feeling "okay." And so we find ourselves completely outside the words of Jesus to Simon the Pharisee, in Luke 7:47: "The one to whom little is forgiven, loves little."

God has so much patience with us, and as much as the other has committed sins that are objectively greater than mine, or has done things to me that I would never have done to them, I know that, nevertheless, before God my nature is the nature of a debtor. I know that it's necessary for me to be in the truth, and I also know that what will really decide my life isn't what the other has done to me, but what I have done.

But, I will say, this isn't even the point. Otherwise we are perhaps still holding a "sin-meter" in our hands, with a mathematical disposition, as there are accounts to pay.

The point is that Christ himself is a happy debtor. God from God, Light from Light, Very God of Very God, is a grateful Son, who never exhausts his joyful debt to the Father from whom he received everything.

Who knows if someone can understand what is expressed by the joy of a child who squeezes their little arms around the bigness of their daddy, and they're happy that he's so much bigger than them? "If you loved me, you would rejoice that I am going to the Father, because the Father is greater than I" (John 14:28b).

Instead, so often, we think like creditors. . . . How many petty-minded people there are who don't know how to contemplate the generosity of life and are obsessed by what they're missing. And by contrast how many people there are to whom life has said very hard "noes," disabled or poor brothers or sisters, who have an astoundingly cheerful and grateful heart that always looks at what their situation is and rejoices in it. How many times has my two-bit faith been humbled by the joy of these sisters and brothers, by people who are sick, by those who are dying: serene debtors in comparison to my sad heart of a creditor.

121

How many people spend their lives in complaining, pointing at others, making the lives of others and their own lives miserable. And how beautiful, on the other hand, are those who, far deeper and humbler, are adept in the art of gratitude and happiness.

The former don't even know where forgiveness starts. The latter are familiar with it, they need it, and they take it as being obvious. "And who am I not to forgive you? If you only knew how much patience God has with me!"

Forgiveness starts with measuring everything in the light of our relationship with God.

## A MARVELOUS STORY OF FORGIVENESS

In Genesis 37 there is a marvelous story of forgiveness that it would be worth reading slowly and that leads to the reconciliation of a man, Joseph, the favorite son of Jacob, with his brothers, who out of envy sold him into slavery, triggering a terrible sequence of tribulations. Joseph, going from one unexpected reversal to another, never interrupts his relationship with the God of his fathers, and step by step he meets with the goodwill of all those who have authority over him, rising to be the prime minister of Egypt. Here, after so much time, his brothers go to ask for bread, not knowing they're asking it of the brother they had betrayed.

It would be very interesting to analyze the process of forgiveness in Joseph, who is led by wisdom: it's a process of growth in which he doesn't "sell" his benevolence, but with a very deep strategy he leads his brothers to remember the wrong they have done, and to redemption through an act of reciprocal love. When Joseph sees a brother who offers himself instead of another (Gen. 44:33–45:4), then he can reveal himself. Their process of reconciliation is mature, and he can then welcome them fully.

All of this account is of an extraordinary psychological delicacy, but what interests us here is the argument that Joseph uses to explain his forgiveness:

"I am your brother, Joseph, whom you sold into Egypt. And now do not be distressed, or angry with yourselves, because you sold me here; for God sent me before you to preserve life. For the famine has been in the land these two years; and there are five more years in which there will be neither plowing nor harvest. God sent me before you to preserve for you a remnant on earth, and to keep alive for you many survivors. So it was not you who sent me here, but God; he has made me a father to Pharaoh, and lord of all his house and ruler over all the land of Egypt. Hurry and go up to my father and say to him, 'Thus says your son Joseph, God has made me lord of all Egypt; come down to me, do not delay. You shall settle in the land of Goshen, and you shall be near me, you and your children and your children's children, as well as your flocks, your herds, and all that you have. I will provide for you there—since there are five more years of famine to come—so that you and your household, and all that you have, will not come to poverty.' And now your eyes and the eyes of my brother Benjamin see that it is my own mouth that speaks to you. You must tell my father how greatly I am honored in Egypt, and all that you have seen. Hurry and bring my father down here." Then he fell upon his brother Benjamin's neck and wept, while Benjamin wept upon his neck. And he kissed all his brothers and wept upon them; and after that his brothers talked with him. (Gen. 45:4–15)

Joseph's argument is sublime: he looks at the story from the perspective of Providence: "Do not be distressed, or angry with yourselves, because you sold me here; for God sent me before you to preserve life. The wrong that you did to me was taken and turned by God in his plan of salvation for all of us." But this unheard-of explanation would be confirmed at the end of the story.

Jacob would go down and would die at the side of Joseph, who was able to care for him, accommodating his brothers as well. Upon Jacob's death the brothers become afraid and say:

> "What if Joseph still bears a grudge against us and pays us back in full for all the wrong that we did to him?" So they approached Joseph, saying, "Your father gave this instruction before he died, 'Say to Joseph: I beg you, forgive the crime of your brothers and the wrong they did in harming you.' Now therefore please forgive the crime of the servants of the God of your father." Joseph wept when they spoke to him. Then his brothers also wept, fell down before him, and said, "We are here as your slaves." But Joseph said to them, "Do not be afraid! Am I in the place of God? Even though you intended to do harm to me, God intended it for good, in order to preserve a numerous people, as he is doing today. So have no fear; I myself will provide for you and your little ones." In this way he reassured them, speaking kindly to them. (Gen. 50:15–21)

Perhaps Joseph says, "I forgive you because I am your brother," or, "I forgive you because I love you," or yet, "I forgive you because I am good." No, he makes God his measure, putting away his rancor, saying, "If you thought you were doing me wrong, God's thought was to make it serve as good."

The assist that we receive from God enlightens our conscience and lets us exercise forgiveness, and only in this way do we welcome the light that puts us in the holy condition of those who are aware of having received much and given back little.

This is how we are able to forgive: living on the generosity of God.

# 6

# BEAR WITH THOSE WHO WRONG US

## (IN ITALIAN: "BEAR PATIENTLY WITH TROUBLESOME PEOPLE")

With regard to the Christian works, we can ask ourselves which is worse, to deny them or to monkey around with them. From what we have seen up to now, it's easy to understand that this writer maintains that it's worse to monkey around with them—that is, to live a Christianity without everlasting life, without the life of Christ, to live out our baptism as belonging to a religion and not as a change in origin of our being, as a rebirth from on high. That's worse, because it doesn't deny Christianity, but it makes it ugly. And therefore useless.

If a young man is in love, he doesn't have to be told to do something for the woman he loves. He does it because he doesn't care how much time it takes: for him to ride on a train for four hours in order to arrive and spend an afternoon with her and then turn around and go back seems worth it and makes him happy. If a person has encountered God in their life, to be with him isn't a rule they have to submit to: it's their joy, their pleasure. And it's natural to structure existence itself and all that's a part of it by seeking the heavenly Father in every act. "For with you [Lord] is the fountain of life; in your light we see light" (Ps. 36:9). But so often this has not happened, and that can be seen in weariness in keeping up with the Christian life. Everything is a bit heavy and tedious, and the Christian works can't be seen, because they're done starting from ourselves, not from the power of God.

The effect is that if a young person is orienting themselves in life and they ask what beautiful thing they ought to do, if they look around where we come from, often the sight they have before them is so substandard. . . . Everybody wants to experience in order to believe, and if we evangelize, how can we think about not being weighed, measured, looked over? The works of mercy are the primary testing ground of a Christianity that's either according to grace or according to human initiative. The first is happy, satisfied, agile; the second is heavy, accusatory, disappointing.

Nonetheless, so many times we try to do "Home Depot" Christianity, based handyman-style on "do it yourself," something done at home in biorhythmic waves.

Sometimes we almost manage to fake these works. But "bearing with those who wrong us" seems rather difficult to me. . . .

Let's be clear: these works, taken in order, have their own crescendo. I will allow myself to say that of the acts of mercy presented up till now, this is the most difficult. We might thing that the preceding one, "forgive offenses," wins that medal and has the highest place on the stand. No, I don't believe so. Forgiveness happens from time to time, and it's limited in scope—very serious, very painful, but still circumscribed.

A person who *continuously* wrongs us, we can bear for a day, a period, a phase. But this is the only work that has an adverb, *patiently*, which indicates duration, continuity.

To stick it out for a time: we can attempt to do that. But to bear with, without solution, continuous harassment, nuisance, disturbance, repeated interruption—these are things that exhaust the most well-intentioned of people who are harassed.

## A WORK MARKED BY CONTINUITY

The Italian word for "bear with," *sopportare*, comes from the Latin *sub-portare*, meaning "to bear up under," while the root of "patiently" is *patire*, meaning suffering that's linked to the fact of being the object of something that makes us suffer. *Troublesome people*, on the other hand, are those people who are particularly burdensome. The Italian word *moleste*, "troublesome," comes from *mole*, a word that can mean "volume" or "bulk," but that's used here in the sense of "grinding wheels," "millstones." This implies that such people are all over us; they weigh on us, they're intolerable. The opposite of this work is impatience, which is something very harmful.

With this work as well we can't cheat, because to bear patiently with a diving bell on top of us, inside of which we cook, but outside we stay calm and peaceful, carries an obvious expression: sooner or later we explode.

As we have mentioned, bearing patiently with troublesome people is a work marked by a characteristic of continuity. Indeed, a person doesn't "trouble" us if they do something just once. But if they repeat it in an insistent manner, this makes us see something important: the extraordinary is easier than the ordinary. "We can be heroes, just for one day," sang David Bowie. In other words, to be heroes for one day, we can do that. But to be one every day—bearing patiently with our colleague who every day has a way of mocking that harasses in a scientific manner—is so, so much harder.

Do you think a marriage blows up over big arguments? No! It's the little daily things, the small stuff, the little irritating habits that cause life's pleasantness to crumble: the feminine manipulations, the masculine individualism, the things said badly, the unwarranted delays, the tiny amounts of discomfort and awkwardness, the inconvenience that the other is. Always. Then the big arguments arise, when they're no longer approached with reciprocal respect, because the other is burdensome, is dull and tedious; because to go back home is to enter something unpleasant, obnoxious. So, we pull the string and give ourselves the right to be neurotic or superficial, and we don't realize how much we do that and how troublesome it is.

The word we should think of is *exasperation*. This word means "to make sour," and it's the condition in which we throw out the sour part. This doesn't come on suddenly. Whether we are patient or impatient can't be verified with a short test, but with the long repetition of harassment.

Troubling people are not those who bother us once, but rather those who repeat these things over and over. They're people who are constant, consistent within themselves, who smash you down regularly, and you are there, smashed down.

How do we attend to this practice, usually? What are the counterfeits of this work? The first—urban, civil, and all the more hypocritical—is *tolerance*. It's up-to-date, modern, politically correct. As my guide in the Ignatian Exercises, the great Fr. Marko Ivan Rupnik, often says, by tolerating we tolerate a poison. In fact, this isn't a big declaration of love: "My dear, I tolerate you." In other words: you are deadly, but I can handle it. Tolerance is a type of killing of the relationship. I understand that you are fatal, and I make myself insensitive to what you are, while waiting for you to finish or to change. However, this doesn't last. When the bearers of politically correct behavior get going, they become ferocious. Because they're in the right, and therefore all means are justified.

Another quite widespread attitude is *do-goodism*. How horrible. I do good; I tolerate you. You're disgusting, that's clear, whereas I'm not. That blank smile that's a living excuse toward everybody. It's often a sentimentalism that transforms itself into disregard and contempt. God save us from do-gooders, from those who pass themselves off as lacking original sin, those who don't love but are better than others. Class-conscious according to an invisible caste, according to the obnoxious karma of giving life lessons to everyone, and thereby making use of either the above-mentioned tolerance or of resignation. Moreover, authentic relationships can't be established with do-gooders, because they're do-good people, not good people. It's a good and beautiful thing to enter into a relationship, dirty our hands and get really mad, and react when it happens. Not stay impassive off and on, little saint statues in somebody's collection. Nonetheless these break out before "tolerant" people, because the religious or moralist pattern requires the punishment of the troublesome person, sooner or later.

Then there is *subservience*. If do-gooders rise up against their neighbor, subservient people spread themselves thin under troublesome people, hoping to find a space for survival between the shoe and the sidewalk. You know how it is—sometimes between the heel and the sidewalk there is about a quarter of an inch. . . . They're gutless, obviously, and faint-hearted. They're also forgiven and welcomed. But they don't pass off their inconsistency as a work of mercy. You don't react because you have the Holy Spirit, but because you lack the guts to do otherwise. Weak toward the strong, and strong toward the weak. Men who don't defend their women. Priests who are devoted to don Abbondio.[20] Bishops who back up the one with whom they're speaking. People without personality, who then, having found someone less powerful than they, take out on them the stored-up violence they have accumulated. It's better if I stop here, I who am intolerant and wicked. . . .

We should not avoid talking about *marpionism*. Sometimes a defeat is a good strategy. Good strategists know how to lose something in order to obtain what they really want. The practice of having two different objectives, of having a plan B, of finding leeway for their own advantage in the crazy things others do. Yes-men who surround the powerful, slimy people who know how to turn the accounts one way or another when the boss changes, those who manage to make a career under every supervisor, those who always land on their feet when the bishop changes. But didn't I say I ought to stop?

---

20  Don Abbondio is a cowardly, hypocritical priest in *The Betrothed*, a historical novel by Alessandro Manzoni. First published in 1827, it is thought to be the most widely read novel in Italian.

But it's also the apparently patient attitude of certain young guys. One of the gravest errors that we make when we become engaged is to start out on the path toward marriage thinking we will iron out the characters, planning to change the people: "Now my boyfriend is so troublesome, but I'll marry him and then watch me work on him!" Mistake. That doesn't happen. People don't change their personality. If they change it, later they wake up as if from a coma. And anyway, if someone changes character, they change their tastes as well, and you can't keep up with them.

But we ought to accept that we have all been weak with these and other weaknesses, because the troublesome person is really troublesome, and trying to pass ourselves off as Christians when we are not in a state of conversion is hard work, and somebody has to do it. . . .

Well, I'm having too much fun. You can't do that. That's not good. After this I'll give myself a good talking-to that I won't easily forget.

## GIVE THE OTHER THE TIME TO REPENT

*Bearing with*, or *sopportare* in Italian, comes, as we have seen, from *sub-portare*, meaning "to bear up under." In the end this brings us to a word that has a similar etymology: *support*. It's something quite different if a friend says to another, "I support you, I bear you up," as opposed to saying, "I tolerate you." The declaration of love mentioned above, "My dear, I tolerate you," which is rather ghastly, is the mark missed by the declaration, "I bear with you; I am on your side." If indeed we link *bearing up* with the simple virtue of human patience, in the end this puts us under a gigantic, absurd strain. Who can bear up under the intolerability of what the other does? We need a completely different root for this act that's so generous.

We need to point out that in our common use in Italian, *bearing with* (*sopportare*) and *supporting* (*supportare*) are not synonyms, whereas they are, etymologically. We understand *bearing with* in the sense of *tolerating*, but it has nothing to do with that. Unfortunately, that's our common understanding, and this is why we go at the work of mercy that turns *bearing with* into *supporting*, sustaining, welcoming the other, in a certain sense being concerned about them; but how have we come to do such a thing? That's a question that we have asked ourselves many times in this work of spiritual mercy.

This work teaches us to recognize a fundamental need in our lives, which is, specifically, *patience*. Let's repeat that this work has one more quality, with respect to the others: its style.

*Counsel the doubtful* is a verb and a direct object. *Admonish sinners* is the same, as are *comfort the afflicted* and *forgive offenses*. But *bearing patiently with troublesome people* has an adverb added—namely, *patiently*, which shows the special feature and the beauty of this work. It makes it clear that we are dealing with continuing, repetitive action, revealing an extraordinary attitude—namely, *patience*.

This needs to be understood better. It's the only attitude that appears in all fourteen of the acts of mercy.

The word *patience* is linked linguistically and logically to the word *patire*: "suffering, enduring." It's therefore the capacity, we could say, of knowing how to suffer.

The Greek in the New Testament uses the term *makrothymía*. In reality, the common meaning that we give to *patience* is, in sum, rather close to the Greek. But in that language, it has a stronger connotation. Let's attempt, then, to deconstruct the word. *Macro* is easy: it means "big." *Thymía* is the feminine of *thymós,* and it indicates the soul, the interiority of humans, the wellspring of feeling, of *being*. More than a spiritual dimension, it has a rather existential significance; it is at the root of our interiority, and it translates into English as "spirit, soul."

In reality, while we use *spirit* to mean the spiritual dimension, by contrast we use *soul* to define something more elementary, something sentimental. The correct term is the literal translation: *magnanimous*; that's exactly what the word *makrothymía* means: of a great soul, forbearing.

This is the first characteristic of love in the famous hymn to charity by St. Paul, in 1 Corinthians 13:4.

So, let's try to understand patience as marking, as we have said, *magnanimity*.

But what does it mean to be magnanimous, to have a big soul?

In English, the synonyms of magnanimity are gentleness, calm, patience, tolerance, generosity, nobleness. *Forbearing* is the first synonym of *magnanimous* found in the dictionary: the "length" of the soul, its greatness.

Let's stop to consider these adjectives: *gentle, calm, patient, tolerant, generous, noble.* When do we have evidence of these qualities? First of all, let's try to see what the opposite is: *aggressive, hasty, impatient, intolerant, greedy, vile.*

So, we have qualities that are, shall we say, of an interior, subjective, personal order, in our relationship with the other. That is, there is no being patient if there is nothing to wait for. We don't have a generous person if there is nothing or no one that needs something. We don't have nobleness of soul if not with respect to someone who would bring us instead to behave in an ignoble manner.

So, we are dealing with a behavior that's an ability. To do what? To give, to the other person, time, space, possibility.

Gentleness shows up in those who don't react violently. Calm shows up as tranquility when faced with something that in itself would give rise to anxiety. Therefore, magnanimity isn't an interior quality, one that inspects itself, but an ability that that makes itself authentic when faced with the mistakes of others. It is, more broadly, the attitude by which we give our neighbor the possibility of repenting, of mending their ways, of turning within themselves, of finding the best of themselves.

The root of all is God. Indeed, we are dealing, and we will repeat this once more, with a work of eternal life, an act that's the fruit that comes from synergy with the Holy Spirit. Indeed, it's one of the fruits of the Spirit in a memorable text of St. Paul, found in Galatians 15:22.

In the Old Testament it's interesting to remember that this adjective, *magnanimous*, is one of the determinations of the quality of God, in the text that we saw in the chapter on mercy in Scripture, in Exodus 34:6, in which God affirms that he's "slow to anger," an expression that was later translated, in the ancient Greek version called the Septuagint, as *makrothymía*.

There is a very beautiful passage in 2 Peter 3:9:

> The Lord is not slow about his promise, as some think of slowness, but is patient with you, not wanting any to perish, but all to come to repentance.

Why does God have this patience? Why does God give us time to repent? Why does God give us space and a means to mend our ways? In short, why is he patient? The answer to this question is less obvious than it could seem at first glance: because time is something he has so much of; time is one of his creations, as is everything.

We don't have patience with our neighbor, because for us time is limited, it has an end. We have little time. One who doesn't believe in eternity doesn't have God's patience, isn't on his side. We are slaves of time, small, limited, weighed down by our anxieties, and then we are impatient; we steal time—we press, push, oppress others when they're weak, when they're fragile, because if we give time, we think we are wasting it, since we don't have more time in exchange.

It's interesting that, in the book of Revelation, the one who is anxious, who is enraged, impatient, is the evil one. The devil, who isn't the lord of time and history, is in a hurry. He has no more time, he's full of fury, knowing that he has little remaining time, time that's numbered. That's the definition of him that we have in Revelation 12:12.

God's patience is his eternity. He has humanity at heart, our salvation, and he grants all the time that it takes to achieve it.

How many times are our assessments debatable, wrong, due to the fact that we are completely conditioned by that creation of God called time. In the same text of 2 Peter that we have just mentioned, in verse 8 we read,

> But do not ignore this one fact, beloved, that with the Lord one day is like a thousand years, and a thousand years are like one day.

God is the magnanimous one, because he has a "nonanxious" relationship with each one of us, not temporal, not temporary, in complete truth.

Time is a creature of God, just like each of us, whereas instead we live in time and are often slaves of time. To be able to give time to others, we need to own it, and in the end, we need to have it. To give abundantly to others, we need to have richness within ourselves.

So, how can we have within us this *makrothymía*, this magnanimity, this greatness of soul, this touching patience of God toward each one of us? How can this become one of our qualities? How can we receive it? It's a question of turning to advantage what we receive, of taking complete possession of the time that God gives us—that is to say, of the scope of God's mercy, of God's patience.

We are patient toward our neighbor when we keep fully present all that God has forgiven us, all the patience that God exercises toward us.

These are reflections that ought to be constantly with us, as is always having clearly before our eyes that God doesn't deal with us according to our sins, according to what we deserve.

If this world were ruled by justice, if it were in the hands of a God who desires to "settle accounts" with us and at a given moment stops giving us other possibilities, none of us would be saved. God doesn't deal with us according to our sins. Instead, there is a part of our soul over which God extends his merciful hand. No person on earth has ever truly seen themselves put completely to shame, even the most reprehensible people in history. There is always a part that God reserves to himself for judgment. Because God is our Father, and a father protects his children.

Sometimes we perceive God as being far from us, but in the absence of initiative on God's part, there is the cry of his patience. This is the silence of a God who watches us with a gracious eye far beyond our appearance, beyond the curtain of smoke that we raise with ourselves and that we use with each other.

This patience of God is something we need to take advantage of. With the measure with which we measure we will in turn be measured. And we need to be a bit careful with saying, "That's enough, I'm not giving you another chance," because the day will certainly come in which we will also need another chance. There is a blank check that God signs for everyone, one that puts us all somewhat in the holy fear of closing the books.

The *makrothymía*, magnanimity, of humankind derives from that of God. This isn't human goodness, nor a quality, nor a capacity, nor an attitude produced by us; it's a memory, a constant act of conscience, by which one such as St. Paul, for example, who by nature was a violent executioner, as he himself says in 1 Timothy 1:13, became magnanimous, patient, capable of giving others another chance. We all live by the second chance that God gives us—and then the third, the fourth, the thousandth.

The Church lives on patience, on mercy. The Church based on patience, on mercy. The entire world is based on that scandalous capacity of God, which he showed in his Son on the cross, to forgive us while we are killing him: "Father, forgive them; for they do not know what they are doing" (Lk. 23:34). Truly, so many times we know little about what we are doing, and perhaps we write ourselves a certificate of good conduct to survive our conscience. We don't remember, as we saw in the preceding chapter, that we are debtors in the sight of God. From the memory of God's patience, there springs forth kindness, slowness to anger, patience toward our neighbor.

What is the characteristic of someone who is magnanimous, patient? Knowing that God is at work. Every person who does wrong makes others suffer, but surely they will come back to themselves about this, sooner or later. We leave to God the role of supreme judge: God, who gives us the authentic, real chance to live with a sense of time that's wide-ranging, not anxious but wise.

God knows where to take us, how to "fix" things. He knows how to straighten out our spirit.

Those who are magnanimous and patient are, however, not ones who remain indifferent. Rather, they seek justice and move in truth, but they do it with peace as their starting point, with patience.

This is a question of effectiveness. A spoken word is effective if it's magnanimous. Magnanimity isn't that which leads to silence about wrong, because if someone is troublesome, they're troublesome, and it's useless to pretend nothing is wrong. Patience leads us to say that which needs to be said, but because the other is my sister, my brother, they're precious; I can't let them go.

We must not speak to a troublesome person in order to get rid of them. It's one thing to tolerate with disdain and disrespect; it's another to watch out lovingly for each other.

## THE TROUBLESOME PERSON, MESSENGER OF GOD

At the beginning of this chapter we remarked that impatience is the negation of this work, and this is true from various points of view; but it's also useful to put our finger on the fact that impatience is destructive. The problem, indeed, is that discerning, edifying, doing truly great things, are things that require constructive behavior that implies *patience*. Can the passage from being troublesome to being constructive be done only by removing the source of trouble? What exactly is this attitude of constructiveness?

The art of edifying, building, is emblematic throughout Scripture. Building the temple is one of the focal points of the Old Testament. In the New Testament there is a matter of building a completely different temple. Let's take a text by St. Paul in the Letter to the Ephesians:

> The gifts he gave were that some would be apostles, some prophets, some evangelists, some pastors and teachers, to equip the saints for the work of ministry, for building up the body of Christ, until all of us come to the unity of the faith and of the knowledge of the Son of God, to maturity, to the measure of the full stature of Christ. We must no longer be children, tossed to and fro and blown about by every wind of doctrine, by people's trickery, by their craftiness in deceitful scheming. But speaking the truth in love, we must grow up in every way into him who is the head, into Christ, from whom the whole body, joined and knit together by every ligament with which it is equipped, as each part is working properly, promotes the body's growth in building itself up in love. (Eph. 4:11–16)

Why are we using this text when speaking about this work? Because what gives us the most trouble in the aggravations that others give us is that they interrupt something we're doing. And then? We try to think that supporting a troublesome person is difficult because they shatter our framework and disturb a project of ours. Perhaps they prevent us from doing what seems to us absolutely to be the will of God. And if this work is sublime, the more difficult it is, the more sublime it is, and also because it touches the deepest of chords in our spiritual growth. In order to love a sister or brother who troubles us while we're doing something "holy," we need to love them more than the thing we are doing. Even if it's holy. And the Church isn't built with projects but with love. (Good grief, will I still have a job after this book, in a

Church that's in love with projects, that smashes the existing in order to affirm the hypothetical?)

What does it mean to edify, to build up?

In Scripture we have the parable of the importunate widow, who is the troublesome person par excellence:

> Jesus said, "In a certain city there was a judge who neither feared God nor had respect for people. In that city there was a widow who kept coming to him and saying, 'Grant me justice against my opponent.' For a while he refused; but later he said to himself, 'Though I have no fear of God and no respect for anyone, yet because this widow keeps bothering me, I will grant her justice, so that she may not wear me out by continually coming.'" And the Lord said, "Listen to what the unjust judge says. And will not God grant justice to his chosen ones who cry to him day and night? Will he delay long in helping them? I tell you, he will quickly grant justice to them. And yet, when the Son of Man comes, will he find faith on earth?" (Luke 18:2–8)

The interpretation of this parable that in this context I would like to offer is the following: I am the judge of life, and the people who trouble me are asking me to grow. People who bother me, those who telephone me at the wrong time, those who mess up situations, those who contradict, those who throw a monkey wrench into the works, are the ones who make me pass from my injustice to God's plan, to doing justice.

We're talking about a curious work, that of transforming troublesome people we've had enough of, those who are certified troublemakers, into emissaries from God, into people whom God sends us, whom he allows to arrive in our lives. Because we who start out as unfair judges turn into generous judges. It's a matter of transforming every troublesome person into an importunate widow; after all, what is a troublesome person asking of me? They're asking me to interrupt the flow of my actions. In fact, what is particularly irritating in the moment in which I'm being troubled is the breaking of my rhythm, my plans, a situation in which we're doing things and the troublesome person interrupts us or causes us to do them differently or even badly.

There is a holy doubt that ought to come into our heads: What if God is using this person? What if God, in order to interrupt the plan of our lives, which is ours and not his, actually uses people who get in our way in order to make us stop going at our own rhythm and go at his? What is God's rhythm? God's rhythm is patience, slowness to anger, as we have seen. Here we are definitely referring to that quality of God: slowness to anger.

We have the rhythm of our show of hyper-efficiency—we have to do things, do things, do things: "I'm doing things, I see people. . . ." And the troublesome people, the people who are faulty, annoying, capable of weighing us down, force us not to be efficient. But is this truly a loss? According to one operative and dramatic point of view. According to the spiritual point of view, it's a holy, extraordinary hand to bend our hearts, because in the end, we get attached to our rhythms, our objectives and projects, and so, very often, the defects of others are emissaries of Providence to bring us down to earth, to reality, to realizing that things will end up well if God helps us, not if we are logical and reasonable and always active.

If the Holy Spirit comes into my heart, what happens? What will the Holy Spirit tell me? The results of a football game? What the weather will be next Sunday? Come on. The Holy Spirit talks to me about the works of God and about God. He's the Spirit of the Son, the Spirit of Christ, the Spirit toward the Father, toward God. We receive the Spirit in order to see how God works in our lives.

The impatient person is the one who doesn't know how to wait. Is there something to wait for in our lives? When something happens in our lives, by any chance is this God's plan? By any chance does God, through secondary causes, remain the primary cause of the whole story? And in spite of all the obstacles, just as billiard balls crash into each other, is there nevertheless a design? Does Providence exist? Does a plan of God exist in our lives? Do things ever get away from the hand of God? God never gives anyone permission to sin. For example, when something bad comes our way from someone, it isn't as if God says to someone, "You have permission to do wrong," because God doesn't give permission to sin, and evil is never something present in his plan. But he knows how to bring life out of evil, to bring life out of the offense; he knows how to pull off how to give something even by means of something harassing.

Does there exist or not a direction in our story? Is life directed by Providence, or does it go on haphazardly?

These are the questions that we ask ourselves in order to see if we possess true patience. We should read St. Paul in Romans 5:3–5:

> We also boast in our sufferings, knowing that suffering produces endurance, and endurance produces character, and character produces hope, and hope does not disappoint us, because God's love has been poured into our hearts through the Holy Spirit that has been given to us.

One who in the midst of suffering enters in the name of Christ knows *patience*, and patience gives the proven virtue in which that which is tested is fundamentally the experience, the discernment, the state of being tried, of having grown—in other words, the adult life. And it comes from the fact of having seen many times what grace God has known to bestow in the midst of suffering. *Patience* is that type of attitude by which we know that despite everything, in spite of human wrongness, God remains the Lord of history and is leading us somewhere. The point is to stop looking at the troublesome person, but rather look at God.

And this is what constructiveness is. This is what building up others is. Not to be the slave of a hypothetical architecture, but in the here and now to build by means of everything that happens to us. St. Maximilian Kolbe built love by means of Nazi savagery. To do this we need the Holy Spirit to speak to us of God. It isn't a problem of consistency; it isn't a problem of skill or of strength! It's a problem of opening up to the work of God.

Speaking personally, God has often placed the greatest graces in the hands of people who have done me wrong. I've been living the experience of the Ten Commandments for about twenty-five years, and if it only stopped this very day, what I've been able to live and to see would be big enough to magnify God, not only for me but for thousands and thousands of people, for all eternity. But what if I were to tell you that it all began because a brother caused me to miss the decisive appointment for my doctorate? If I tell how I experienced a violent rage toward that troublesome brother who, not carrying about our agreement, blew out from under me the planning of my studies at that moment? There was a correspondence between the Secretary of the Pontifical Biblical Institute and the then Cardinal Vicar of Rome. I was to be a teacher and dedicate myself to studying. But that brother knocked me out of everything. I found myself free for a month, an entire September. And I attempted to think that perhaps this was a mercy.

I remember indelibly when the Lord extinguished the rage in my heart by means of James 4:13–15:

> Come now, you who say, "Today or tomorrow we will go to such and such a town and spend a year there, doing business and making money." Yet you do not even know what tomorrow will bring. What is your life? For you are a mist that appears for a little while and then vanishes. Instead you ought to say, "If the Lord wishes, we will live and do this or that."

That was in the summer of 1993. In September, with my doctorate having been knocked out for the moment, very shortly afterward I took the kids to two retreats. The most important ones that I had ever done. They were the first two groups of the Ten Commandments.

I love that brother. He did me good. There are so many people to whom good things have happened, thanks to him. I ought to tell many other stories, but it would be complicated to lift the curtain of smoke without revealing the defects of some people. I can just say that troublesome people have always done me good. The greatest graces of my life have been brought to me by them. And the battle has always been the same: to get past my intellect in order to arrive at Providence.

## GOD'S "RHYTHM"

Is God there, underneath my story? Is God underneath what happens to me? How many times do we become hard, ferocious, nobody can talk to us, because we have in our heads an objective and we don't see any other? God in his mercy has provided for mortals to be free, and this implies that in the world there can be sin, and that sin comes upon us, and often through the hands of another person. The Lord Jesus Christ received evil and restored it as a gift. We, on the other hand, take evil as a mistake to be avoided, to toss aside, and not as a way to be like the Father, who is patient. Many times, we frustrate God's plan for us. We push away the Holy Spirit, we neutralize the grace God gives us. But he recalculates the course once more, setting off again on the road to save us all the same, in spite of our opposition.

Indeed, we need also to think of how troublesome we are to God, how troublesome we are to Jesus Christ, to the shepherd who has to stop letting the sheep graze, leaving the ninety-nine sheep in order to go searching, while blowing his projects to smithereens, for the sheep that was lost. He has to go after her, take her on his shoulders. That sheep is troublesome, but what a joy it is to find her again! That's what God is made of. He takes interest in finding us, interest in carrying us on his shoulders. When Christ experienced trouble from us, he entered into the Father's design and purpose, and saved us.

*Patience* isn't passiveness; it isn't resignation, but it's capitalizing on the pain and the concrete suffering, building on it so it becomes something. Waiting. Look, *patience* is to say, "I'm waiting for something so important that I can get through this as well," and accept a cost for something that's very beautiful: being able to suffer with a view to something.

> If any want to become my followers, let them deny themselves and take up their cross and follow me. For those who want to save their life will lose it, and those who lose their life for my sake will find it. (Matt. 16:24–25)

Taking up our cross is the second act. The first is to deny ourselves, to deny falling in love with our own thoughts, to accept that what we think isn't an absolute, to be free from our designs and plans for ourselves. To be free from our own life. In Greek, *psyche.*

Without a doubt, the greatest preacher in Scripture is Moses. There is a whole book, Deuteronomy, in which we read four very long speeches by Moses. He keeps talking, talking, talking, but we need to remember that Moses was a stammerer.[21] The people of God were there, and they had to receive the Word of God from a person with a speech difficulty! Think about that! But if you have the patience to sit and hear what he says, he spoke with God, and up to now no one has ever spoken that way. You could say it in a quarter of the time, but you would never say that. . . . Slow and immense, or fast and bland? You tell me. . . .

---

21 But Moses said to the Lord, "O my Lord, I have never been eloquent, neither in the past nor even now that you have spoken to your servant; but I am slow of speech and slow of tongue" (Exod. 4:10).

What does this mean? That God's "rhythm" isn't mine,

> For my thoughts are not your thoughts,
>     nor are your ways my ways, says the LORD.
> For as the heavens are higher than the earth,
>     so are my ways higher than your ways
>     and my thoughts than your thoughts. (Isa. 55:8–9)

Sometimes there exists another troublesome, and, so to speak, holy thing: if in life we have encountered some persons who carry out something very holy and very good, persons who serve the poor, who help the marginalized, we have very often found ourselves facing people who are insistent, nagging, who so much love the poor people with whom they're concerned that they never let go and insist until they get what their poor people need. These are people who know how to be troublesome to the point of opening hearts. Many times, we have met people who are so tenacious in doing good that they go so far as being troublesome, so as to obtain, perhaps from powerful people who are quite indifferent, a good thing for someone. Don Oreste Benzi, a saint of our times in my humble opinion, is an example of a gentle but insistent person.[22] He pleaded and begged for the poor women he freed from the oppression of prostitution; he pleaded for help and he got it. In his blessed battles he was wisely, gently, mercifully troublesome. He knew how to bother people until he got what he was looking for: that's troublesomeness that's holy and opportune as well.

In the end every one of us has had to accept that someone who was asking strongly for something from us was right in asking us for it. In the end it was a beautiful thing that this person interrupted the course of our days. A child knows how to bother us, but it's also right for the

---

22  Oreste Benzi (September 7, 1925–November 2, 2007) was an Italian Roman Catholic priest and the founder of the "Associazione Comunità Papa Giovanni XXIII." Benzi championed the rights of the individual and founded his association to aid teenagers in their lives and their path to Jesus Christ while also striving to evangelize to those including the destitute. The cause for sainthood commenced in 2014 under Pope Francis, and he's titled as a Servant of God. See https://en.wikipedia.org/wiki/Oreste_Benzi.

child to do so: they're a child, what should they do? They should look for our attention! Young people know how to be troublesome, but it's right for them to be so: they're looking for parenting, care, someone to watch out for them. They're looking for wisdom, and it's right that they ask it from us. Let's hope that they don't grow weary of asking us for it, and that they don't become discouraged if they find we give them a cold shoulder.

There is a beautiful phrase from Francis of Assisi: "So great is the good that I am expecting that every trouble is pleasure for me."[23] The trouble that I find in my path is downright pleasant, because I know that it will bring me good.

When is it that a troublesome person is unbearable? When I lose sight of the good toward which I am headed. When the troublesome person is tolerable, can I bear with them? When I don't consider them irrelevant to the good that I am pursuing. What good? What are we journeying for? If we said first that our problems are our plans that are shattered, this means that we have our projects, our plans at heart. Then it's to be understood that the only thing that's worth having at heart is . . . our heart. Its capacity to love.

We live to learn to love; this is the fundamental task of my existence. I was born to know, love, and serve the Lord in this life and in the next and to let myself be loved by him. On Chiara Corbella's tombstone there is written this marvelous sentence: "The important thing in life isn't to do something but to be born and to let ourselves be loved."[24] I was born to love, so it isn't irrelevant for me to challenge the fact that someone bothers me, hinders me, is troublesome to me: this is really the testing ground; it's actually the path on which I grow. I want to have patience in order to bear with people, but the reality is that unbearable people teach me wisdom. They're in the basis of the growth of my heart if I decide to grow.

---

23 Franciscan sources tell us that Francis of Assisi said this to St. Leo on May 8, 1213.
24 Chiara's inspiring story is told in Simone Troisi and Cristiana Paccini's *Chiara Corbella Patrillo: A Witness to Joy* (Manchester, NH: Sophia Institute Press, 2015).

If my waiting is properly directed, what am I waiting for? The moment when I'm on my own and finally I get to rest and to do my own thing? Or am I waiting to reach the goal of loving others and losing myself by truly loving? If what I am waiting for, if my patience is in with that goal in mind, the idea isn't so intolerable for someone to put me to test, someone who exasperates us a little: building love implies patience. We live in a "use and throw away" mentality, in which things have to be immediate and without duration. But love can't be like that. Love is faithful, and God's love is eternal. Our love aims to become that.

Love is stable, it's undissolvable, it's wholly love—not only love between spouses: every relationship, if it's true, is undissolvable and isn't subject to being broken. Every friendship is undissolvable if it's true. Every fellowship is undissolvable if it's true. But this requires patience, not the utilitarian logic of exploitation. This is true as well for creation, as Pope Francis spoke splendidly about in his encyclical *Laudato Si'* on ecology: humanity exploits the world instead of taking it as a gift and as an occasion of love.

We must go into depth, that depth that's the center and the truth of our being: we were born to learn the art of true love. Troublesome people are perfect teachers, living instructors.

To win a game it's best for an athlete in training to be put into serious difficulty. We are like that: Are we to love like Jesus Christ and then complain if we aren't given the opportunity? God in his mercy has given us the gift of our troublesome people. Let's keep them close, because if we lose them, we also lose the way of love.

# 7

## PRAY TO GOD FOR THE LIVING AND THE DEAD

How many times, when I've taken young people to become acquainted with cloistered convents, during the times of dialogue with the nuns, have I heard them ask: But doesn't it seem to you that enclosing yourselves in here is a waste of time? In the world there are a boatload of problems, so what are you doing here? Why waste your lives in such a useless way?

It's impressive how this type of affirmation/question seems quite "social" or "supportive," but it reveals, in reality, an individualistic view that materializes in thinking that we start out and go save the world just to suit ourselves, according to our own whims, more or less.

And in that case, we truly waste a lot of time and energy. Through disorganization and unilateral action. Actually, the good is in itself much broader than the activity of a single person.

I've heard the nuns reply by often giving the same example: But do you know that the Church is a body? Do you know that we are all of us united? Each one of us is part of the same mission. Do you see that Fr. Fabio evangelizes? But do you know that Fr. Fabio is nothing without us? You see your hands moving and doing "useful" things, but do you know that you have a heart in your chest that, if it stopped beating, your little hands actually do nothing? Do you know that there are people behind Fr. Fabio who keep him on his feet and who will never talk to you, but who help you by means of Fr. Fabio?

One time I sent a young woman to ask for her certificate of baptism from her parish—a document that would be useful for taking a testing time in a convent. It was as if this were the first time this had ever happened: the priest went on a tirade on the uselessness of convents. One thing I knew for sure: that priest doesn't pray, or he does it so badly that he doesn't know how urgent it is.

If the things I do don't start out with prayer, they'll become gray, in black and white, transparent, without depth. Because I haven't touched my heart, and above all, I haven't let it be touched. And I become a practitioner. God save me! And especially may he save the people of God from a priest who doesn't pray.

Christ saved the world. Yes, but after thirty years of silence. And even when he had started traveling around stirring things up, he would take irritating blackouts:

> In the morning, while it was still very dark, he got up and went out to a deserted place, and there he prayed. And Simon and his companions hunted for him. When they found him, they said to him, "Everyone is searching for you." He answered, "Let us go on to the neighboring towns, so that I may proclaim the message there also; for that is what I came out to do." (Mk. 1:35–38)

And it fell to Simon to leave his home, Capernaum, to go wandering about.

Jesus didn't move if he didn't start out with prayer. And in prayer he discovered his "elsewhere," his direction. To be firm in order to be able to start out. His entire mission started out with forty days of prayer. And before the most important things that he had to do—suffer, die, be buried, and rise again—he initiated everything in Gethsemane. Not to plan. Not to gear up. To dialogue with his heavenly Father.

And he prayed for me on the cross. The man who made a mark on history more than any other, did it in a sublime uselessness. On the cross, without any movement allowed. There's nobody more useless than someone like that. We say: my hands are tied, I can't do anything. He was nailed down. And he saved the entire world.

## TALK TO GOD ABOUT PEOPLE

The last of the spiritual works of mercy, therefore, is "Pray to God for the living and the dead." How does this ever show up last on the list? Why is it the least important? Normally, in the dynamic of faith, the last is the point of arrival, the goal.

As we saw, instinctively we move as if to give ourselves to prayer is surely a noble activity, but, with a practical spirit, not about things, we see it as less urgent or less efficient with respect to the other works of mercy. Our hyper-efficiency and our thinking of ourselves as God Almighty lead us to act, resolve, move . . . and instead of sitting still and speaking with God . . . well okay, later, sure, I can hardly do it, sure, for certain, wait till I get there, in the meantime you start, because here there are problems to solve.

But this work is the "over and beyond" of the other works. Why? The works of mercy are to serve others, and the spiritual works, at least four out of seven, are for talking to other people about God. But so many times this isn't possible. We don't manage to do it because we don't have the conditions, or because it really is useless: the other person doesn't listen to us and doesn't welcome what we say. Then we often need to move from talking to other people about God to talking to God about other people.

Indeed, we need to emphasize: here we are not talking about generic prayers. Someone might think that here we have an opportunity to address prayer as an act in itself. No, the argument is this: pray to God for the living and the dead. Here we need to talk about the specific prayer of intercession. It's interesting to recall a phrase from St. John Chrysostom: "To pray for oneself requires need, whereas to do it for others stimulates brotherly love."[25]

Nevertheless, we can pray for others without charity, without heart, in a distracted way, as happens many times when we formulate prayers in congregational prayers, which can be grandiloquent. For example, we pray for peace in the world, but this is an aesthetic act, representative stuff.

25  John Chrysostom, *Homily on Matthew*, 14.

Actually, this work enumerates, among its substitutes, a peculiar imitation: prayer isn't contrasted only with "non-prayer," but also with superficial prayer. Prayer requires love, and love is a movement from me to the other that in this case passes as dialogue with God. Let's think of how many times we have distinctly perceived prayers as a superficial, formal reality.

This type of work has a strange characteristic: it's invisible. It isn't a work that gives an acknowledgment, a relational attestation, like the others. If I pray for you, you don't see me doing it, and vice versa. And so it happens that we promise each other that we will pray repeatedly for something. Does everyone pray for others as we say we will? Is it cynical to doubt that? Or is this realistic?

Why is love necessary for prayers of intercession? For two motives: the One whom we are beseeching, and those for whom we are interceding.

First of all, we are not praying to an entity. We are not presenting a bureaucratic instance that sets off a procedure, etc. God guard our hearts, and may he never give us a bureaucratic instance that kindles a procedure, etc. "Ask, and it will be given to you; seek, and you will find; knock, and it will be opened to you" (Lk. 11:9). The emphasis in this sentence from the Gospel is in the first part: ask. If you don't ask and you don't knock, how can anything be given to you? To ask is to beg, plead, entreat, and at the same time it's to believe that the other has the power to hear and grant our requests. In this the text implies some serious things: sincerity, faith, forward movement, constancy.

If we look at the distraction with which the repetition of formulas of prayer drag on among the Sunday faithful. . . . There ought to be people who speak energetically with the Almighty; better still, there ought to be an army of children who, with unshakable trust, ask their good Father about this, in the way children who want something from their mother or father nag them until they get it.

We need to think of prayer as being a paradoxical contest with God. In Genesis 32:23–33, for example, Jacob wrestles all night with Someone who, in the darkness, he doesn't manage to see clearly. Little by little he comes to understand that the adversary is God himself. And he comes away from that night both weakened—because he has learned his limits—and strengthened, changed, matured: and in fact, he changes his name to "Israel," nothing less. This is a key episode in the Old Testament. Here he appears as the Patriarch par excellence, the man who became familiar with the profound nature of a relationship with God and who reveals the importance of the seriousness of prayer. About this episode Benedict XVI in fact said,

> Prayer requires trust, closeness, almost a symbolic hand-to-hand combat not with a God who is an enemy, and adversary, but with a God who blesses. . . . For that reason the blessed author uses the symbol of a wrestling match, which implies strength of soul, perseverance, tenacity in attaining what he desires.[26]

So we are talking about the combat of prayer. The Church says,

> Prayer is a wrestling match. With whom? With ourselves and with the cunning tricks of the tempter, who does his utmost to divert people from prayer, from union with their God. We pray in the same way we live, because we live in the same way we pray.[27]

Instead, the prayers of the faith are often read in a tone that earns the same share of attention as a dissertation on the extinction of ground-walking birds in lower Angola.

This is due in part to our liturgical slip into a Pavlovian state of affairs, with conditioned reflexes, an act of having our minds somewhere else, whereas our bodies and tongues react as if saying nursery rhymes, with our inner involvement being comparable to the stand-by light on

---

26  Pope Benedict XVI, General Audience, May 25, 2011.
27  *Catechism of the Catholic Church*, 2725.

a television set. The Mass begins, and everybody starts out and does things together, one after the other after the other, wherever we come from. In the middle there would also be specific prayer for our brothers and sisters and for the whole world. But what really was said? Did we pray for people stricken by earthquakes? Are you sure? I don't know; I wasn't paying attention.

But our state of trending toward individualistic self-centeredness, which is much more worrisome than the drift of formal liturgy, leads us to observe the problems of the other people around us and others in the world, with cold distance. The television news while you are eating, the facts about the world as the generic background of the context of life. At other times, on the contrary, there is a sentimental, occasional participation by the surface of the heart, but it isn't something that truly touches us. Or rather, not in a lasting way. It passes out of our mind and we don't even remember it.

The tragedies of others are food for curiosity, not existential, personal questions we ask ourselves, demanding an answer.

The point is that for prayer we need love, because graces come through love. And what we ask God for has no better channel: the world is saved by love. And all the beautiful things that we must do on this earth, if we do them without love, are unwatchable, cold. We need that which makes us go beyond doing things only to say we did them to doing them truly and with our hearts engaged.

The problem, therefore, is that this work requires something quite noble in the depths of our existence. It requires us to start from the innermost parts of our being. To pray to God for the living and the dead means to forget ourselves and to center all of our own attention, our desire, on our need for the other, on consideration for the other that's expressed by an act that has no acknowledgment, no visibility, for which perhaps no one will say thank you to us.

## A WORK THAT FLOWS FROM OUR POWERLESSNESS

This work, then, is founded on a relationship that goes toward God and has regard for other people. This action flows, if it does flow, when we are conscious of our powerlessness, when we discover that we can do no more—as if prayer were a small thing. But in reality, this is where we reach the heart of all the works that we do.

Let's take the case of parents. Parents have many things to do for their children. Fatherhood and motherhood involve concrete and objective care, so all these works can easily be understood in a parental role.

Parents give food and drink to the hungry and thirsty ones who are their kids, whom they welcome and clothe because they arrive naked and need to be protected, housed with care, attended to when they're sick, helped when they're trapped in their fears. How much advice there is to give to children, how many doubts to confront, how many beautiful things to teach them, how many mistakes to correct with love, and how many times must they be comforted and encouraged, and have their trust restored. What a beautiful calling!

And then parents will need to forgive them over and over. And God alone knows how parents can hurt a child. And how troublesome children know how to be! How much patience you parents need to have! And you do have it. You get it.

But there comes a time when you, dear parent, discover that you can't do anything for your child, because the child won't listen to you any more, can't stand you, accuses you of things that you can hardly even understand; you've become useless to them—they push you away.

Worse, the day comes when a father and a mother discover that they could do something, but they shouldn't do it, because the child has to grow, has to be independent, needs to have their freedom respected, otherwise they remain big babies. So many people refuse that day and don't pass to the later phase: accepting that they should not do anything for the child any more.

On that day you can pray; in that moment you can and should go out and say prayers, fast, give alms for your child, without telling them.

Pure love, pure doing it without any compensation, in which parents go all the way to the end. And this implies a healthy, objective relationship, with our helplessness. We have limits; and this implies opening up to prayer. But for this we need a sense of God, a sense of his power, bowing our heads before something that only he can do.

So often we would like to convince the hearts of people, and we know this isn't within our grasp. We can only offer our heart to God. And woe to us if we don't do that. Many times, by not having given ourselves to prayer, we've forced things. We should have given ourselves to prayer, but instead we've inundated the doubtful with words, badgered the afflicted, exasperated those in error, confused the ignorant. Out of haughtiness we've continued to say and do things that we should not have done, while we should have stopped where we belong and, in secret, raised our hands, not in giving up but in prayer: "It came about when Moses held his hand up, that Israel prevailed" (Exod. 17:11).

How difficult it is to accept being a creature. Prayer is an act that's typical of the creature toward its Creator, of one who is little toward its point of reference, of a limited and mortal being toward what is the fountain of life—what are we in the face of the Eternal One?

Many times, we don't make it to this work, because we don't accept saying, "Here I'm finished," "Here I'm stopping." So many times, we ruin our lives through interventionism.

Let's understand each other: I'm not saying that we can't do everything we ought to do, or that we ought to be geared toward doing the least possible. We need balance in everything, and logically also in this. Actually, there is another paradoxical imitation of this work: praying for someone when we could do something for them. That also is absurd.

To think that we could set out to solve a problem for a person and instead to say, "I'm praying for you." Obviously, it's better to do something for them. What is required here is a sense of reality, a nobleness of perception, a sense of the measure of things, that only charity, of the true kind, can give.

We can pass from distracted prayer to the opposite, reaching the point of interventionism, but there could be a balanced position: loving prayer that has asked itself if it could still do something, and when it accepts that it has encountered its limits, it becomes a cry toward God, a pleading, and a relationship with him.

In that sense we ought to be mindful: all this implies faith. And all this is essentially linked with one aspect of the gift of baptism: in the prerogatives of our baptism there is the common priesthood of the faithful.

There are those who are ministers of Christ's priesthood, those who are ordained, the priests; but in reality, every Christian is a priest, and can intercede for the whole world, can intercede for all people. We know that the Church lives on prayer, because it lives on a hidden, beating heart that supplies to all its parts this relationship with God.

We began by remembering that reply of the cloistered nuns to the young people who at times I bring to meet them. It's beautiful to quote this text from St. Thérèse of Lisieux that inspires that reply:

> At prayer time my desires were making me suffer a true martyrdom, so I opened the letters of St. Paul in order to look for some sort of answer. Chapters 12 and 13 of the first letter to the Corinthians fell under my eyes. I read in the first of those chapters, that *everyone can't* be apostles, prophets, teachers, etc.; that the Church is composed of different members, and that the eye can't at *the same time* be a hand [1 Cor. 12:29, 21]. The answer was clear, but it didn't fulfill my desires. It didn't give me peace.
>
> Just as Mary Magdalene, who kept bending toward the empty tomb, ended up finding what she was looking for [Jn. 20:11–18], in the same way, abasing myself even as far as the depths of my nothingness, I raised myself so high that I was able to reach my

goal. Without becoming discouraged, I continued my reading, and this sentence gave me relief: "Now eagerly desire the greater gifts. And yet I will show you the most excellent way" [1 Cor. 12:31]. And the Apostle explains how the most *perfect gifts* are nothing without Love . . . and that Charity is the *excellent way* that leads surely to God. Finally I had found rest.

Considering the mystical body of the Church, I had not recognized myself in any of the members described by St. Paul, or rather, I wanted to recognize myself in *all of them.* Charity gave me the key to my *vocation.* I understood that if the Church had a body composed of different members [1 Cor. 12:12], it was not missing the most necessary, the most noble of all: I understood that the Church had a heart, and that this Heart was *burning with Love.* I understood that Love alone can cause the members of the Church to act. If love were to be extinguished, the Apostles would no longer preach the gospel, the Martyrs would refuse to shed their blood. I understood that *Love* contains all the Vocations, that Love is all, that it embraces all times and all places . . . in a word, that it is Everlasting!

Then in the excess of my delirious joy, I cried out, "Oh, Jesus, my Love . . . I have finally found my vocation: My vocation is Love!

"Yes, I have found my place in the Church, and that place, my God, You have given me. In the Heart of the Church, my Mother, I will be *Love.* That way I will be everything . . . that way my dream will become a reality!!!"[28]

St. Thérèse, the patron saint of missions, of evangelization, is a woman who never left her convent, died young, prayed, and knew, by having perceived it in the key moment of her discernment, that the heart of everything is love, and that being in contact with love is vital for the salvation of the whole world, and for the Church.

---

28   St. Thérèse of Lisieux, *The Story of a Soul,* trans. Robert J. Edmonson, CJ (Brewster, MA: Paraclete Press, 2005).

## THE SUBSTANCE OF ALL THE OTHER WORKS

It's worth repeating: in this work we find the substance of all the other works, because prayer for the living and the dead is the unseen aspect of all the other works. After all, let's try to think of what the other works become if they don't come from prayer.

On thinking carefully about this, venturing into that journey, we were mindful to enumerate the imitations of the spiritual works of mercy. And these imitations, if we look at them in depth, had a constant source, and always started from the very same root: the absence of relationship with God. And consequently, they were clumsy mimicry that lacked in depth.

When there is no heart behind the act that I am performing, it's because there is no prayer. Because I am starting from myself and not from God. And what I offer is mediocre. It has no everlasting character. Because what comes from me has no everlasting character, and I won't get it by the sledgehammer of volunteerism. Mercy is the richness of God, not mine.

We can give food to the hungry or drink to the thirsty without mercy. Is that possible? This is really the fundamental theme of 1 Corinthians 13:1–3, which was so cherished by St. Thérèse:

> If I speak in the tongues of mortals and of angels, but do not have love, I am a noisy gong or a clanging cymbal. And if I have prophetic powers, and understand all mysteries and all knowledge, and if I have all faith, so as to remove mountains, but do not have love, I am nothing. If I give away all my possessions, and if I hand over my body so that I may boast, but do not have love, I gain nothing.

I could give my whole body, give away all my goods, but without love. I don't need love to do the works concretely. To do them, I just do them. But it's important to see how.

157

I could clothe the naked, but I could do it without giving them dignity, like an automatic dispenser, while the one who clothes you is always a little like God after sin entered the world (Gen. 3:21), who sews garments—the image is of an infinite tenderness—for Adam and Eve, who were ashamed. He's a Father who covers his weak children. I could give lodging to pilgrims like an innkeeper, without asking myself if I've hosted them truly in my heart, without being at home with them. I could visit the sick in order to feel at peace with my conscience because I had not yet gone to find that sick person; that makes me look bad, by not entering into the other's pain, discharging the duty and going away when the quota of embarrassment has reached the maximum level of sustainability. I can visit those in prison but remain a stranger to their condition. Or do it in a condescending way.

The most emblematic is the corporal work of burying the dead. What kind of thing is it to bury the dead without praying for the dead, or without believing in eternal life? This is an attitude of undertakers, doing a physical work without the sense of loss of the person, simply *putting a person in a grave.* Is this called "ditching them"?

We can't do the corporal works of mercy without the seventh spiritual work of mercy.

And we also can't do the other six spiritual works of mercy without the work of prayer. Let's think about counseling a doubtful person without having prayed, without having first been certain about God, whom we need in order to speak with the doubtful person, and without having entered into their doubt in order to understand their plight.

Let's think about what it can be to teach without praying in our hearts, without love behind it. This means beating the other on the head with facts without caring for their greater good, for their heart.

Let's think about what the admonition of a sinner without prayer is: we see so many people who have to reprimand their neighbor—they have to make their point, tell "the truth." The question begs to be asked:

But are you praying for the person that you need to admonish? But are you ready to fast for that person, to give alms—multiple times—for that brother or sister? But do you truly pray for that person? Then, if you haven't prayed, keep quiet: it's better for you not to start doing that act of talking superficially to the other person; what you are after can't be done by one who isn't a disciple of the merciful God.

And the same is true with forgiving offenses: this can be done as an act of simply recovering our own peace, an act of taking care of our own problems. Often people actually brag about forgiveness; they think they've achieved forgiveness, but instead they've simply displaced their attention: there is no prayer and love for the other.

And in the same way, bearing patiently with a troublesome person can be done by making the time pass while waiting for the other to disappear, leave us in peace, and not as a personal inner journey in which I grow in the patience of love. That inner path can result only from the One who is patient, slow to wrath, rich in grace, full of mercy.

## ONLY LOVE CREATES

If the works of mercy aren't born out of intimacy with God, if they aren't born out of the secret between us and God, then where do they come from? What could they ever be? They will only be horizontal philanthropy, limited in the sense of justice and of our own perfectionism, and they'll have no depth; they won't touch the secret. The corporal and spiritual works of mercy need the invisibility of prayer. If I don't come from the connection that gives me love and which is to enter into the relationship of the Most Holy Trinity, and if as a son I don't ask the Father for that love that is the Holy Spirit, then what can I start doing after that? In the relationship of the Trinity each Person causes the other to stand out, and that's true love, the parameter on which to base the work. Christ intercedes with the Father, and the Holy Spirit reveals him to us.

Where do the corporal and spiritual works of mercy come from? Our whole journey has been understood as a sort of "customs clearance" of the works of mercy from the horizontal to the vertical, from the visible to the invisible, from the simply human to the human touched by the divine, from our stammering attempts at charity, which is a theological virtue and a gift of God. It entails passing from what we improvise by ourselves to what God can do in us, and only he knows how, because if he doesn't do it, all these works can be surrogated to our do-goodism, activism, and perfectionism.

Prayer is an act that doesn't compare to the others. It's a secret; it's an intimate place, or at least it should be. If in that secret there exists our relationship with our neighbor, and if our relationship with our neighbor is in the sight of God, then when we come to our neighbor, we bring God. That is, if I deal with God with respect to others, with others I will deal with respect to God. And what I do, perhaps without needing to chat and campaign, becomes an announcement of glad tidings; it becomes evangelization, because I'm proceeding out of love—I'm proceeding out of the reality of the invisibleness of God.

"Only love creates!" are the words that St. Maximilian Kolbe said before being interned in Auschwitz. How true that is: not only does love conquer hate, but it also gives marvelous form to all that we undertake.

We must remember a fundamental thing in the Christian life. The *thing* isn't paramount; *how* is paramount.

The most decisive thing is that we do things with our hearts.

Acts can be grandiloquent, but so can the pomp of the world; but these deceive the world and don't come from God.

Our works can also be small, but they can arise from the Father and from the freedom of our inner selves.

Then they save the world. Because they give it zest.

But we asked ourselves a question here and there in the other works, and why not ask it here, too? If the other thirteen works emerge from the fourteenth, where does this last one spring from? Where does prayer flow from? How do we arrive at prayer? Where does a true cry toward the Eternal break out from? Simple: from anguish, from distress, from heartache.

What? From where? From poverty, from our limits, our helplessness, from need, from heartache, as I've said. Or rather? God gave us the gift of anguish to acknowledge that we're insufficient, that we need him, that we don't have everything wrapped up, that we must ask for help.

But we defend ourselves from that anguish, from that heartache; we seek to circumvent it by becoming dazed and alienated.

But we need to ask the question in a better way: Where will a prayer for our living and departed brothers and sisters emerge from and be sincere? Well, it's about seeking out the anguish that brings us to a cry for help. It has to do with a somewhat bitter labor: making our hearts reach out to the other's pain. Beholding it and not flipping by it, as if changing a TV channel. Staying with it, focusing on the loss.

When your heart hurts for someone who has gone through a loss or who is suffering, pray truly for that person. You can't sleep, you don't think about anything else, you feel a deep sense of pain, you feel the tears that are on the brink of being shed. Yes, you pray, entreat, implore. And you are ready to give up what is yours in order for God to help that person.

Love doesn't spring from a full stomach. Love doesn't spring from comfort. Love springs from the bitter draft of your limits, which, if you don't resist, become an open door to be loved in your weakness and then open your eyes to the weakness of others and feel its weight, its suffering. Then follows concern, caring, from one weak person to another.

The mercy of God seeks out our poverty and loves it.
And our poverty, once it is loved, becomes mercy.

# ACKNOWLEDGMENTS

This book is due to the perseverance of many people who insisted that I write it. To all who remember saying to me in some way that I ought to undertake this thing, I give my thanks. So as not to hear you go on any longer, I spent my two and a half weeks of vacation doing this. And you were right. You did me good: I wrote it on the boundary between rest and prayer.

In the draft the young people who come to the Journey of the Seven Signs[29] helped me, transcribing the catechism and the broadcasts. And special thanks to the indispensable principal supervisor of this text, Fabrizio Fontana, who helped me in everything, especially with the draft, in a wise, graceful, and enriching way.

I must also thank my collaborator, Elisabetta Palio, who often calls me out and is patient with my rough character.

So as not to offend anyone, besides these two I am not thanking anyone else explicitly—and so I am sure to offend many others. It's a question of functional democracy.

---

29  The Journey of the Seven Signs (*Il percorso dei sette segni* in Italian) is a time of Christian formation offered to young people who have completed the Journey of the Ten Words. The purpose of the Journey is for young people to travel through the seven signs of the Gospel of John and thereby to learn the fundamental keys for entering into a personal relationship with God the Father, and to receive all the equipment they need to confront the challenges of a Christian life.